A Leader after

GOD'S

Own Heart

Combining leadership principles from the private sector, military, and the Bible to make our culture and world a better place to live in.

CHARLES CROUCH

ISBN 978-1-0980-9526-0 (paperback)
ISBN 978-1-0980-9527-7 (digital)

Christian Faith Publishing
832 Park Avenue
Meadville, PA 16335
www.christianfaithpublishing.com

Printed in the United States of America

CONTENTS

ADMISSION

Why This Book Was Written

Let's start things off by addressing the elephant in the room. As an ex-Navy SEAL, I am presumed guilty of using my trident for, what some might call, "cashing in." This is often an unspoken assumption in a room, left unaddressed. Even though I draw from my experiences as a SEAL, this book is about so much more than that. It is about human leadership experiences, which even someone without the military experience who has a heart for a godly lifestyle and leadership should stretch for and attempt to obtain. Just so you know, I tremble with fear as I try to put on paper what God has put in my heart through seeking Him.

This book was written because I can't stay silent as I watch so many people stumble and fall over themselves as they reach for higher goals. My hope is that out of the thirty-one principles I lay before you, you can grab a few golden nuggets from which you progress to the next level. I hope to be a part of your success. I hope you are catapulted to better ways, better leadership, and a better life.

There is a void in the market of 'good' leadership. The word you may have just read over there, "Good," has been used much too often and without definition or context. For example, some might think that "good leadership" is a CEO that doubles or triples the value of a company, or another leader that accomplishes X, Y or Z goals. No, "good," means leaders are taught to bring out the "good" in others. I see too many employees who do not appreciate their bosses and conversely, bosses who do not appreciate those they lead. It is a sad thing because bosses should be motivating and inspiring to their employees every day. If you think your boss should change for the better, then silently hand them a copy of this book.

When I sat down to write this book, many pointed out Navy SEALs have already written books on leadership. They said, "Charles, it's an overcrowded and already saturated market. Why would you write about it again? Why not just write about something else?"

My response was yes, there are many leadership books written by Navy SEALs, a group of men who are notoriously aggressive, creative, forward thinkers, who have a history of achieving difficult tasks. These men have much to say about society in general. I am one of them. What many of them have written has merit. However, the leadership book before you, what you will read here, is my attempt

to steer society in a right and good direction which inspires members

of my, your—OUR—community to do their fair share part in lead-

ing us into the future.

Elephant confronted, let's get after it!

FOREWORD

Why me? Why now?

I spent five years as a Navy SEAL. Navy SEALs are one of the most elite fighting forces in the world. I was deployed and served in battle. I have lost friends, many of whom believed the fight we were engaged in was worth the ultimate sacrifice. I have witnessed brilliant leaders who inspired greatness and vision in myself and others. But I have also seen poor leaders who did not understand their role and leaders who failed those who following them in battle, business, and life. Good or bad, there surely is be a better way.

The Higher Ground

Historians and experts have formally studied the strategies of war from ancient times to today. There were many brilliant leaders who conquered worlds with varying styles. One strategy was important to all of them. High Ground.

High ground is an area of elevated terrain, which can be useful in combat. The military importance of the high ground has been recognized for over six thousand years, citing early examples from China and other early dynastic cultures who regularly engaged in territorial/ power struggles. Later, castles and fortresses, which included towers and walls were designed and built on high ground, and would provide structural advantages for positions of troops and weaponry deployed, thrown or fired from above.

In 2006, the United States rewrote the Army and Marine Corps' counterinsurgency manual. Despite the revisions, the new strategy centered on a familiar principle that transcends centuries of war: taking the high ground.

Historically, in conflicts, the high ground was considered the most advantageous place to be on the battlefield. The high ground was an elevated piece of terrain, such as a hill or a mountain from which a unit could best defend themselves and see approaching adversaries. It was an advantage, in many ways.

However, in some arenas, this strategy does not hold true. Just as in the revolutionary war where we out witted the royal army on our turf by using terrain to hide, we have to keep changing the way we think in our ever-changing world. We cannot battle an al-Qaeda-type enemy the same way we battled the Germans in World War II. Sitting atop a hill, despite superior firepower, is no longer an advantageous position. In fact, it is counterproductive when fighting an insurgency or an enemy who blends in with the local population.

The revisions to the counterinsurgency manual argued that the "high ground" in this new type of conflict is not any type of terrain, but rather it is the indigenous people. In order to win this "terrain," we have to come off the hill and immerse ourselves in the community. We need to create relationships with the local people, understand their fears and needs, provide security, and we must win their hearts and minds.

The same is true today of leadership principles, and in business, and in life. The high ground in your career battles should be the people in your following and the local community. Win this "terrain" and you will have the information and opportunities needed to figure out the best next step in your life and career.

One profession highly associated with the idea of leadership is politics. But it seems many politicians are still using an old style of leadership. Many politicians, as evidenced by today's campaigns, do not seem to recognize, or accept this truth. Politics and the election process have become a series of micro-aggression campaigns against the other side instead of standing for something, presenting ideas, and ultimately working together to provide balance. In an outdated act of "taking the fort," politicians seek to divide our communities into separate categories to win a majority of votes.

I love that we Americans have freedom of speech. I have fought for that piece of paper called the Constitution. Sometimes, I dislike what people do with their freedoms like tearing down their fellow man, but I respect their rights under the Constitution. Many use their freedom to tear their perceived so called "enemy" down. Truth be told, both sides do it. Red and Blue. Conservatives and Progressives. Republicans and Democrats. The rules of the game are archaic in nature and the code of conduct has been forgotten.

This is an unfortunate reality present in democracy and in many other places around the world. Even though being "against" a thing or someone can win an election, it prevents real change or conversation or compromise from happening. This falls under the umbrella of poor leadership.

America was not always this way. There was a time when we Americans stood up for what we believe in, a time when we were willing to fight for a moral cause, no matter the cost. A time when we didn't scare so damned easy. We became great by daring great things.

An example of this was over two hundred years ago when fifty-six men signed their names to a document that would change the course of human history.

These men were of varied backgrounds, ages, education, property, and experience.

Twenty-five were lawyers. The next most numerous were merchants (twelve) and landowners (nine). There were four physicians, two farmers, and two full-time politicians with no other occupation. Benjamin Franklin was the only printer.

The document they signed was, of course. The Declaration of Independence.

Sixteen of the signers had not voted for independence when the vote had been taken on July 2nd but later did agree and sign the Declaration.

Eight of the signers were declaring the independence of a land in which they were not born, and all eight of these were natives of the British Isles.

These fifty-six men did not agree on everything. There were political differences. But when the fate of the country was in the balance, they publicly declared their commitment to the "self-evident truths" that formed the foundation of our nation that "all men are created equal and endowed by their Creator certain inalienable rights that among these are life, liberty and the pursuit of happiness."

They did not only sign their names and send others out to fight. Over a fourth of them—seventeen—saw military service during the revolution. Four of them were taken prisoner. Nine of the signers, all of whom had pledged their lives to the support of the Declaration, would die during the revolution.

Most of the signers, politically sophisticated and living amid eventful times, did not in their later years, dwell on this historic moment when they had signed it. They did not write memoirs of the event or, for the most part, even refer to it in their letters.

In doing a job that had to be done, they set their minds toward change and then took the effects of their actions in stride. The final sentence of the Declaration of Independence is a promise among the signers, to "mutually pledge to each other our Lives, our Fortunes, and our Sacred Honor."

As I reflect on the courage it must have taken to publicly sign their names to the Declaration of Independence, I cannot help but think the best way to honor this courage is for each of us to make a similar personal pledge to ourselves, our families, and to our fellow countrymen Americans to grasp and uphold the awesome freedoms they gave us as an inheritance.

Fast forward now to modern times. During the 2018 Global Leadership Summit in Chicago, Illinois, it was said that leadership boiled down is defined as simply *getting people from point A to point B*.

But this GLS definition about leadership does not satisfy me. Why, because it is like saying a sheet of paper is two-dimensional, while everyone knows there is a micro depth measurement being overlooked. A sheet of paper is not a two-dimensional object, it is a three-dimensional object.

Like the thin depth measurement of a sheet of paper, I believe it is the small things that produce life changing leaders—small things like appreciation, empathy, and generosity, which when considered in totality, amount to much more than a small thing for those we lead.

I firmly believe the kinder, gentler America written about in language almost like an epitaph for a time that has died—a nostalgic America—is still alive.

Fundamentally, I believe most people are honest and caring and would lend a hand in a crisis to a friend or a neighbor, and sometimes even a stranger.

Politically, I believe we all agree over more issues than those over which we disagree. When it comes to health care, we all want a functional program. We all want a good economy. We all want peace. Many of us desire strong borders. We all desire honest news and all to be held to justice. We all want a functional system. I would challenge anyone who disagrees to a fourteen-hour debate.

America is lost in the roar of tempers and accusations and empty promises. But it is still there. I see it every day in the small town I live in. It is in the expressions on the faces sitting next to me at church. It is what my wife and I talk about in the evening as one day ends and another begins. Tempers and accusations carry the desire for political power, not the desire to allow people to heal and thrive.

This book is meant to remind me as I write it, and you as you read it, of what makes someone a leader. There are many books that propose to teach you the 10 things, or 4 steps, or 115 characteristics of great leaders. Many of these have their place and offer ideas of merit, but I believe the real information on how to lead is already inside you. This book is meant to remind you of who you are, who you want to be and to offer ways by which you will reinforce behaviors that inspire and empower. It is to remind you to build lives and careers that matter.

We need to retake the high ground of 'good leadership'. The position of honor, service, and integrity. We need to remember the golden rule. And we need to remember, every day, that this life is a gift for which we owe a debt to those who follow us. First for the leader, then for the led.

Further, we must stand in a perspective of faith. The most important element in your role as leader. We must realize, acknowledge and understand that when one dies and stands before Almighty God, we will give an account for what we have done or failed to do. I will also attest that following biblical principles is the most lucrative business and life building strategy on earth. There is nothing else that can produce the greatest return on investment (ROI) under the sun. I would bet my life on it.

What is leadership as a Christian? First, let us contemplate why God created leadership in the first place? And further, why does God make some people leaders, and other followers?

As soul searching as these questions are, one cannot consider these questions without first considering this seemingly parallel of leadership yet foundational question we must ask.

To understand leadership, we must ask: why did God make money?

Take a second and contemplate this fully.

One could argue God created money to test the heart of man. When you, or I, or anyone stands before God, I believe we will each give an account for what we have done and what we have failed to do with many facets of our life, including our money. (Ecclesiastes 12:14). Man having possession of a thing, like money, is a quantifiable way for God to measure our trust in Him. Do you trust Him or don't you? Have you tithed to God, or did you rob Him? Do you give to the poor? The answer to these questions is known only between you and God, but I challenge you to contemplate them.

You see, God gives us things to test us, and come Judgment Day we are accountable.

Now, with that as a foundational structure to build upon, let's go back to leadership.

Why does God make leaders? Again, I believe the answer is to test man. You may be thinking "is everything a test to you?" but stick with me and let's break it down. We are each given something to steward, not just money, but people—our subordinates, friends, family, and often those we encounter for the briefest moments. And again, as for our stewardship, we will one day account for what we have done and what we have failed to do, and even still, it does not stop there. We are to act as influencers through leadership. You see, if you're willing, leadership in all of its iterations, proves to be godly evangelism saving souls.

You are the light of the world. A town built on a hill cannot be hidden. Neither do people light a lamp and put it under a bowl. Instead, they put it on its stand, and it gives light to everyone in the house. In the same way, let your light shine before others, that they may see your good deeds and glorify your Father in heaven. (Matthew 5:14)

In an effort to explore the many ways in which leaders succeed and fail, we will go to the Bible directly, where Old Testament kings provide examples of both the ramifications and rewards resulting from their terms.

Jehoshaphat	Rid the land of male shrine prostitutes. But did not remove the high places and the people continued idol worship there.	1 Kings 22:41–46
Jehoram	He had built high places on the hills of Judah and had caused the people of Jerusalem to prostitute themselves and had led Judah astray.	2 Chronicles 21:11
Ahaziah	He caused Israel to sin just like Jeroboam.	1 Kings 22:52
Queen Athaliah	Mother of Ahaziah, who upon her son's death took the throne. She counseled her son to do wickedly.	2 Kings 11:1-20 2 Chron 22:3
Joash	Left the high places installed and the people continued to offer sacrifices and burn incense there.	2 Kings 12:3
Amaziah	Caused Israel to commit the sins of Jeroboam.	1 Kings 22:52
Azariah	He was righteous, but the people still sacrificed on the high places.	1 Kings 15:4

	Attribute	Verse
OT King Saul	Didn't have patience, enacted taxes, and led his officials not to trust the Lord.	

David	Was a man after God's own heart; left Solomon an inheritance.	
Rehoboam	Led Judah to do evil in the eyes of the Lord. Lost the treasures of Jehovah to the King of Egypt.	1 Kings 14:19
Abijah	Grew in strength, size, and might.	2 Chronicles 13:21
Asa	Built up the kingdom for the people.	1 Kings 15:20–24

Jotham	The high places, however, were not removed and the people continued to offer sacrifices and burn incense there.	2 Kings 15:4
Ahaz	Rejected God, sacrificed his son in the fire, ordered priests and officials to erect idol worship and other altars.	2 Kings 16:4 and 15
Hezekiah	Good, removed high places and destroyed idols.	2 Kings 18:3
Manasseh	Led the people into more sin than the surrounding nations.	2 Kings 21:9
Amon	Led the people to follow the same ways of his father.	2 Kings 21:21

Josiah	Found the Torah buried in the temple. Instructed the officials, priests, the people, and himself to turn back to God and destroy idols.	2 Kings 22:13
Jehoahaz	A mist in the wind.	2 Kings 23:31
Jehoiakim	Led people astray in the ways of his fathers.	2 Kings 23:37
Jehoiachin	A mist in the wind.	2 Kings 24:9
Zedekiah	Led the people to sin just as his predecessors did.	2 Kings 24:19
Ahaziah of Israel	Caused Israel to commit the sins of Jeroboam.	1 Kings 22:51–52
Joram	Decided to join different wars by listening to man and not God. He and his men were endangered and wounded.	2 Chronicles 22:5-7
Jehu	Jehu destroyed Baal worship in Israel. However, he did not turn away from the sins of Jeroboam, son of Nebat, which he had caused Israel to commit—the worship of the golden calves at Bethel and Dan.	2 Kings 10:28–29

Jehoahaz	Caused Israel to commit the sins of Jeroboam.	2 Kings 13:2
Jehoash	Continued in and caused Israel to commit the sins of Jeroboam.	2 Kings 13:11
Jeroboam 1	Created his own festival days for the people; only God could do that. Instituted anyone to be a priest that wanted to; only Levites were to have that position.	1 Kings 12:32
Nadab	He caused Israel to commit the sins of his father.	1 Kings 15:26
Baasha	Caused Israel to commit the sins of Jeroboam.	1 Kings 15:34
Elah	Led others to get drunk.	1 Kings 16:9
Jeroboam 2	Caused Israel to commit the sins of Jeroboam.	2 Kings 14:24
Zachariah	Caused Israel to commit the sins of Jeroboam.	2 Kings 15:9
Shallum	Assassinated Zechariah and reigned six months.	2 Kings 15:10–12
Menahem	Caused Israel to commit the sins of Jeroboam.	2 Kings 15:18

Pekahiah	Caused Israel to commit the sins of Jeroboam.	2 Kings 15:23
Pekah	Caused Israel to commit the sins of Jeroboam.	2 Kings 15:28
Hoshea	Last king of Israel before the exile to Assyria. Sinned liked all the others…but not as bad.	2 Kings 17:2 and 22

Zimri	Zimri caused Israel to commit the sins of Jeroboam.	1 Kings 16:19
Tibni	*History books called him Man of Straw or The Pretender. was overtaken by Omri.	1 Kings 16:21
Omri	Caused Israel to commit the sins of Jeroboam.	1 Kings 16:26
Ahab	Caused Israel to commit the sins of Jeroboam and set up Baal altars in the temple. Erected Asherah poles.	1 Kings 16:29–33

You may have noticed that a king by the name of Jeroboam committed some sins that influenced and were carried by many other kings after his death. So first, who was he, and what were the sins of Jeroboam?

Jeroboam was the first king of Israel during the divided kingdoms of Israel and Judah. He was an effective leader, popular, and charismatic. Yet he erected idols in Israel to give the people something to worship so they would not have to travel to Jerusalem in Judah. You might call this in some ways replacement theology. He appointed priests from outside the tribe of Judah for much of the same reason of keeping people local. He depended on himself and his cunning ability instead of God's promises. His bickering with sister nation Judah led him to keep his people from traveling there. His leadership led the following kings of Israel to follow the same sins and worse.

A king is an influencer of people. God is after men and women who lead others to follow Christ.

Question for you: Who did Jesus go to meet while he was dead in the tomb for three days?

Answer:

For as Jonah was three days and three nights in the belly of a huge fish, <u>so the Son of Man will be three days and three nights in the heart of the earth.</u> (Matthew 12:40). So Jesus went to those in Hell and preach the gospel of the salvation of the Lamb of God to them as an atoning sacrifice. This is only fair as before Christ, there was no gentile atonement for sins, only for the Jews.

This is a big deal if you can grasp what was done, check it out also in Ephesians and Peter.

But to each one of us grace was given according to the measure of Christ's gift. Therefore, it says, "When he ascended on high he captured captives; he gave gifts to men." (Ephesians 4:7–9)

Now what is the meaning of "he ascended," except that <u>he also descended to the lower regions</u>, namely, the earth in which he went and proclaimed to the spirits in prison, to <u>those who were disobedient</u> when God waited patiently in the days of Noah while the ark was being built. (1 Peter 3:19)

So check this out. Jesus went to save those who sinned before their knowing about the book of Law or the Messiah, basically from Noah and back. The Bible **DOES NOT SAY** that Jesus went to preach to the followers of corrupt kings of the OT. You see, they made their choice. They cannot claim negligence. A sad thought when you consider their eternity. Note 1 Peter 3:20. Again, Jesus' atoning sacrifice was for the gentiles previous to the crucifixion, not the rebellious Jews previous to the crucificixion. So, the leaders of Israel who led others to sin, to whom can they cast the blame? To nowhere or no one. Also, to those who were led by evil kings with 'bad leadership', to whom can they cast the blame? To nowhere or no one!

Jesus said to his disciples: "Things that cause people to stumble are bound to come, but woe to anyone through whom they come. [2] It would be better for them to be thrown into the sea with a millstone tied around their neck than to cause one of these little ones to stumble."

(Luke 17:1–2)

You see, it's us leaders. Leadership is a big deal to God. Leaders effect the trajectory of others. We are God's harvest. We are God's portion. Bad leadership robs God of his people in many ways as well as robbing people of a good life. My heart is for you is to excel in the ability to lead others in good things. What is that you ask? Great question, that's what this book is all about. Encouraging leaders to lead others in a good direction, not simply from point A to point B.

The overarching cry of my heart in this book is, 'Let my people go'! I want employees and followers to be set free from blind leaders who care more about ROI than the hearts of those they lead. If you have a boss that needs help as a leader, hand him a copy of this book.

Let's get after it!

CHAPTER 1

Integrity

Language matters. It is at the heart of communication and understanding. It is the way talk show hosts rant and rave about a topic. It is what false leaders use when they make promises they cannot keep, hoping no one will remember.

It's the words chosen for the lyrics of our national anthem that stir us. In an age when news confronts us every minute, the lyric "the *bombs bursting in air, gave proof through the night that our flag was still there*" remind us of a time, and a people, whose dreams and lives were represented by a tattered flag.

Let me just tell you quickly that I actually carry a large amount of integrity—said everyone all the time.

The word integrity is tossed around a lot these days. Almost every politician claims to have extremely high integrity. Every athlete claims to follow the rules. Every corporation claims to have the best ingredients in their products. Integrity has become a common household word used much too loosely.

The dictionary defines integrity as "the quality of being honest and having strong moral principles; moral uprightness—of being whole and undivided." Some people say integrity is doing the right thing when no one is looking. I would also add to that definition one little amendment that makes all the difference; **INTEGRITY IS DOING THE RIGHT THING WHEN THE RIGHT THING GETS HARD.**

When you are "whole" and consistent, there is only one you. You bring that same you wherever you are, regardless of the circumstance. You don't leave parts of yourself behind. You don't have a "work you," a "family you," and a "social you." So what does it take to be someone who leads with integrity?

You're the same authentic person regardless of the situation. You can meet this leader with their family, friends, church, or at a boardroom, and you will see a consistency in behavior, actions, and words.

A leader is conscious of how his/her behavior and words makes an impact on those around them intentionally and oftentimes, unintentionally. When this leader behaves in a way that is out of integrity, he/she stops, acknowledges, apologizes, and corrects course.

Someone with integrity focuses on the development of character. This leader spends time reading, getting coached, listening to the counsel of others, going to leadership development courses, and reflecting on how to develop character.

A confident leader invites others on the same journey. He or she aims to walk in integrity, and as others see it, they are drawn to this. They can have confidence in this leader with the belief that this leader will do what he/she says and believes.

THERE'S A CHANCE THAT MANY LEADERS TODAY, WHEN THEY SPEAK OF INTEGRITY, ARE ACTUALLY COMING FROM A PLACE OF PRIDE, GREED, OR EGO.

When people work high-level jobs that allow them high-level access to secure parts of the government, it can produce pride. A feeling of "I'm above the rest and the rules don't apply to me."

Military Side

As a Navy SEAL, I experienced the way pride stirs into the mind firsthand. You are given authority to do secretive things which can encourage an entitled mindset. EVEN A LITTLE DOSE OF THIS PRIDE DEGRADES THE TOTALITY OF INTEGRITY. The thoughts of pride and elitism go straight to the brain like a fresh injection of CRACK into your veins. Once you feel it, you don't want to let it go and integrity becomes extra baggage that gets in your way. This feeling isn't just among some of our military greats though.

For example, I have seen an ATF agent disregard the speed limit because he believed if he did get pulled over, he could flash his badge. I have seen other high-level military members disobey laws because they do those things in the military all the time.

The same is true for corporate executives who understand finances and tax laws so thoroughly, they cut corners and work every loophole available. Some of what takes place is illegal. It is a combination of greed and pride that pushes them do it. This is not okay, and in 100 percent of the cases you are not above the law. And the problem isn't just the lawbreaking. The problem is the mindset and pride that makes someone believe they are above everyone else. One day, this will cost more than what was gained from it.

Marketplace

Case Study—Matt Kuchar

Professional golfer Matt Kuchar won the Mayakoba Golf Classic in November of 2018. He paid his caddy the $4,000 agreed-upon amount with a $1,000 bonus because of his win.

David Giral Ortiz, who filled in as Kuchar's caddy during the tournament in Mexico, had requested a total of $50,000; Kuchar earned $1,296,000 for the victory, and caddies are typically paid a percentage. (I also read that he requested 10% which would have been 130k but was finally given 50K, a more respectable amount but not what he had agreed to.)

When social media began criticizing Mr. Kuchar, he initially defended the $5,000 payment as fair. When fans at his next tournament booed him, he reconsidered and issued a public statement.

"I let myself, my family, my partners, and those close to me down, but I also let David down," Kuchar said. "I plan to call David tonight when I'm off the course to apologize for the situation he has been put in, and I have made sure he has received the full total that he has requested. For my fans, as well as fans of the game, I want to apologize to you for not representing the values instilled in this incredible sport. Golf is a game where we call penalties on ourselves. I should have done that long ago and not let this situation escalate."

Biblical Perspective

The Bible's perspective, one of the topmost tiers of leadership concerning integrity, can lead to a long list of items for a leader to establish in his or her heart. Look at Joseph fleeing Potiphar's house.

No one would have seen him, that's integrity. Look at David who had multiple opportunities to avenge King Saul, but he didn't. The examples are many, and I would list them but in all reality you and I and everyone already knows how to act in integrity. What I want you to know is how important it is to you and your life. Check out the list of many bible verses.

Similarly, encourage the young men to be self-controlled. In everything set them an example by doing what is good. In your teaching show integrity, seriousness and soundness of speech that cannot be condemned, so that those who oppose you may be ashamed because they have nothing bad to say about us. (Titus 2:7–8)

The integrity of the upright guides them, but the unfaithful are destroyed by their duplicity. (Proverbs 11:3)

To do what is right and just is more acceptable to the Lord than sacrifice. (Proverbs 21:3)

Better the poor whose walk is blameless than the rich whose ways are perverse. (Proverbs 28:6)

Keeping a clear conscience, so that those who speak maliciously against your good behavior in Christ may be ashamed of their slander. (1 Peter 3:16)

Whatever you do, work at it with all your heart, as working for the Lord, not for human masters. (Colossians 3:23)

So you must be careful to do everything they tell you (the Pharisees). But do not do what they do, for they do not practice what they preach. They tie up heavy, cumbersome loads and put them on other people's shoulders, but they themselves are not willing to lift a finger to move them. Everything they do is done for people to see: They make their phylacteries (Old Jewish religious accessory) wide and the tassels on their garments long; they love the place of honor at banquets and the most important seats in the synagogues; they love to be greeted with respect in the marketplaces and to be called 'Rabbi' by others. (Matthew 23:3–7)

Jesus is expressing that what is done on the outside isn't worth anything in heaven. What is done when no one is looking is what's valuable. This is only the tip of the iceberg when it comes to the integrity character piece. Integrity is doing our best in every moment and when we do make a mistake, owning it, apologizing, and making amends.

None of us get a pass when it comes to integrity. None of us are perfect. ALL OF US CAN GET BETTER AND ALL OF US CAN ACTUALLY THINK WE HAVE INTEGRITY WHILE NOT ACTUALLY HAVING INTEGRITY. Thing is, without the real 'do the hard thing' integrity is necessary to becoming a good leader and making sure you don't have a time bomb ticking in your career or life. Working with integrity is the first steppingstone to becoming a good leader.

Activation

Think about your own funeral. Someday in the future. Think of your friends and family who will probably be there. Write down what you would want each of them to say about you. Be specific. Be bold. Write as if you have been a faithful partner, a close friend or business associate. When you are done, read them over. How many of them have to do with money, and how many have to do with integrity of character?

CHAPTER 2

Wisdom Versus Impulse

There are certain times in a person's life when carrying out a plan requires more than education and professionalism, when experience matters, but alone, is not enough. There are times when the decisions we make impact our lives and the lives of many others around us. It is these times which require wisdom.

There are many definitions of the word wisdom, but I suggest that the truest definition is elusive and evading, ducking, and dodging like a boxer in the ring. Most online dictionaries say that wisdom is a combination of experience, knowledge, and good judgment. Apparently, if we roll them together, we have wisdom. I'm not convinced this definition is a bull's-eye because there are so many areas of life where we must stive to carry out a plan for our lives with wisdom.

Let us simply define wisdom as *the application of knowledge today*. When a person uses what they have, that's wisdom. As with intelligence, there can be varying degrees of wisdom from person to person and from day-to-day.

How do we really dig up everything we have in our brains and apply it to the situations of the day? Here is an example, if we have a dog that retrieves the mail, but every day we go over and pick it up, that's not using our knowledge as a dog owner. Wisdom would tell you to take the time to daily invest in training the dog to achieve a result of retrieving the mail.

Let me ask: is wisdom elusive and difficult to nail down, or is it a black-and-white matter? Sometimes I just want to jump up and yell at the top of my lungs and rip off my shirt because wisdom is fleeting; it ducks and weaves like Muhammad Ali, demanding your attention. It's here and there and everywhere yet hidden. With reverence, I believe there are two levels of wisdom. Let me explain them as JV and Varsity.

FIRST, JUNIOR VARSITY: OBTAINING WISDOM AS A PERSON WHO CAN CONDUCT THEIR OWN PERSONAL LIFE EFFECTIVELY.

SECOND, VARSITY: POSSESSING WISDOM FOR OTHERS, A LEADER CAN AND SHOULD INFLUENCE OTHERS TO ACT IN WISE WAYS, SOMETIMES AS AN EXTENSION OF THEMSELVES.

Consider this. We can read all the books and watch all the videos about how to swim, but to actually swim we have to get in the water. That's experience. We cannot understand what is required to stay afloat until we jump in the pool and feel what it's like to move in the water. We cannot experience and know how the water moves between our fingers while treading water if we stay on the shore. Or how the cold water initially takes your breath away. You must experience it first.

Like swimming, doing something wise for ourselves is great and has to be learned over time. To act on wisdom at a personal level and through time, we get better at making wise decisions. Wisdom comes from experience. Sometimes the greatest wisdom comes from the greatest missteps and the pain we create in our missteps. Wisdom rarely comes from education, but usually the street or marketplace. **YOU SEE, EDUCATION ONLY TURNS INTO WISDOM IF YOU APPLY IT.**

We have come to live in a risk-averse world. Failure is not acceptable. And with more to do than ever, and less time to get it all done, wisdom often collides with our choices. Wisdom and choices can be foes of one another in this modern world all too often and we resort to fighting the fires that are the hottest or the easiest to put out, not necessarily focusing on the most important—the wisest—choices we could make.

Younger people grew up with all this business. The digital world has overtaken the real world in the last ten years. Texts replace conversations. Virtual reality replaces actual experience. Skydiving in VR is not the same thing as staring out of the plane door, wind in your face, with the ground thirteen thousand feet below you. In the same way, knowledge gained quickly isn't wisdom.

Marketplace

A friend of mine who owns multiple businesses uses an interesting method to hire managers. He challenges them to a game of chess. He figures after one game, he can tell a lot about the person. He can see if they are aggressive, offensive, shy, or defensive in one game. My friend knows that if they were too offensive, he would have a manager on his hands that would require restraint at times. If they were defensive, he would have to push that person to be proactive in managing the various things involved in a day. By the way, this can be accomplished by playing almost any strategy game.

Military Side

Case Study—George Washington

Wisdom takes many forms. Consider George Washington, the first president of the United States.

He acted in wisdom many times. And with integrity. Wisdom almost always flows from integrity. Why? Because a person who is wise has also probably learned to be humble as well. If we are being dishonest or manipulating people, we will be found out.

George Washington was offered the kingship of the new America after the Revolutionary War was won. The Continental soldiers came to him to make him the new king of the land. He thought it over, said no, and turned around to walk away.

He was one of a few men within the founding fathers to see and know what the colonies were to become and represent, a democracy. He turned down the highest office in the land to let it grow, as it had to, painfully. He knew they were to be a people who represent themselves. For the people and by the people. He understood how a king could misuse his power.

George Washington's <u>wisdom applied to the future of the United States.</u> Washington could conceive of what our country could be a hundred of years in the future. When they built the capitol building in Washington, DC, they constructed a burial place for his body in the middle of the building underneath the famous center rotunda. He adamantly refused it as a burial place because he felt as though people would recognize him as their leader and not themselves. Today his body rests at his farm in Mount Vernon, Virginia.

Biblical Perspective

If you don't read the scriptures, you're missing out on some of the greatest stories ever told. In the Old Testament, King David (the one who slew the giant Goliath) had a son, Solomon. The kingdom was given to him at twenty years old.

He asked God for wisdom, and God gave it to him. A notorious situation he faced proved this to be true. He was asked to make a judgment over two prostitutes. These two women came to him one day and were blaming each other vigorously. The first woman approached the king and explained their arguments.

She and the other women both had baby boys at about the same time. She stated her cause, blaming the other woman. She said the other woman had been holding her baby boy while sleeping and rolled over and suffocated him during the night. She awoke and noticed her baby not breathing then switched the babies without her knowledge while she was asleep. In the morning when they both woke, she thought she had killed her own son in the night.

When the light came in, she saw that it wasn't her own boy but the other woman's. The first woman explained that the second had switched the dead boy for the living child in the night and asserted the first woman had suffocated the boy while her son was still alive.

The two women erupted in argument, each claiming to be the mother of the living child. At this, the twenty-year-old king demanded silence. He had to award the correct woman her son, but how could anyone know for certain which woman was the boy's rightful mother?

KING SOLOMON BLUFFED. UNBEKNOWNST TO EVEN HIS ADVISERS. He asked that the living boy be placed on the table in front of him. He then drew his sword and said, "Neither woman will have the living child, but each one can have half." He then raised the sword above his head to appear as though he was going to chop the child in half. Really, he was watching both mothers' reactions. One woman jumped to cover the child. She yelled, "Don't harm the boy. The other woman can have him." It was in this that she had passed his hidden test.

Solomon then awarded the child to her and exclaimed the real mother would not want her son to be harmed. The story of the young king's wisdom spread, and his popularity grew.

Case Study—Abraham Lincoln

Another leader whose wisdom helped others was our sixteenth president of America: Abraham Lincoln. He is most recognized for abolishing slavery and how he was able to maneuver dangerous political ground to make slavery a thing of the past. His actions parallel the game of chess.

In chess, one must think multiple moves ahead and must position pieces strategically, over time, to win the game. PRESIDENT LINCOLN WAS ONE OF THE BEST REAL-LIFE CHESS PLAYERS IN HISTORY. He had to wait to make a move until the current state of reality was in a certain place, and played many moves ahead.

When Honest Abe first ran for the US Congress, he ran with the campaign promise to end slavery. He lost terribly because no one wanted to side with him on the issue. It was too extreme. America was not ready for it. Lincoln, himself, wanted to make Blacks equal to Whites, but he learned a lesson from his loss and knew he couldn't run for president with the same campaign promise.

He would not have been elected if he ran on the same ticket promises that he did when he ran for Congress. Although that was his unstated goal, he arranged his policies and speeches to slowly move the people's opinion in that direction.

Here is how he did it.

First, Lincoln framed the slavery issue as a national issue, not as a state issue. He argued that "America should be either one thing or another thing." He forced many of the states to align with him. The states divided on the issue which in effect triggered the civil war. Frankly, had he not been elected, there might not have been a civil war. Each state may have remained with the power to keep or end slavery.

Second, when the war was declared and raged on, he passed the Emancipation Proclamation while there were no southern votes to be counted in Washington, DC. He used the absence of Southern senators and congressmen to pass antislavery legislation without pushback. Now, to pass this proclamation, he promised that he would colonize all Blacks outside of the country in Panama. Again, that was a political move, not really what he desired.

Third, Lincoln asked free Blacks to fight in the war. After he did this, he never mentioned colonization again. Ever. Yet the Emancipation Proclamation stood, and Blacks helped the war effort.

Fourth, once reelected, Lincoln declared voting rights for the slaves. I would argue that if he had finished his second term, there might not have been a need for the civil rights marches of the 1960s. But Lincoln's vision was ended by his assassination, squashing his step-by-step march toward recognizing the equality of races.

WE CAN SEE THAT WITHOUT TAKING EACH NECESSARY STEP, HE WOULDN'T HAVE BEEN ABLE TO TAKE THE NEXT STEP. He had to abolish slavery in this way because he wouldn't have been able to win the election had he proclaimed his end-time goal.

How can we use this wisdom to play chess in our own professional and life goals?

I would suggest that all those examples of wisdom come from different dimensions of time but relate to us today.

- King Solomon used his wisdom of other *people* to find truth in the *present* time (street smarts).

- Abraham Lincoln used a game like wisdom to arrange his pieces in the *present* to move the political ball down the field.

- George Washington's wisdom came from a vision for the *future* to walk away from being a king and robbing the people of a democracy.

WISDOM AND INTEGRITY ARE TWO OF THE BASIC INGREDIENTS IN GREAT LEADERS. ONE DOES NOT EXIST WITHOUT THE OTHER. Both take courage and awareness. Both take lifetimes to learn and improve and share.

Biblical Perspective

Let's look at an interesting story from the Bible about the application of wisdom. King David, a man after God's own heart, used what he knew about people to elicit a certain outcome from people. Street smarts.

One day David fled from Saul and went to Achish king of Gath. But the servants of Achish said to him, "Isn't this David, the king of the land? Isn't he the one they sing about in their dances: 'Saul has slain his thousands, and David his tens of thousands'?" David took these words to heart and was very much afraid of Achish king of Gath. David, fearing the King of Gath, pretended to be insane in his presence; and while he was in their hands he acted like a madman, making marks on the doors of the gate and letting saliva run down his beard. Achish said to his servants, "Look at the man! He is insane! Why bring him to me? Am I so short of madmen that you have to bring this fellow here to carry on like this in front of me? Must this man come into my house?" (1 Samuel 21:10–15)

Hopefully, that made you laugh a bit like you just watched a 007 movie where James Bond was able to escape a suspenseful situation.

BUT KING DAVID APPROACHED THIS SITUATION WITH WHAT HE KNEW ABOUT MEN AND APPLIED IT. THAT IS WISDOM.

Now, let me ask this, what does the following verse imply about wisdom and knowledge?

By wisdom, a house is built, and through understanding it is established; through knowledge its rooms are filled with rare and beautiful treasures. (Proverbs 24:3)

Something to ponder more, but King Solomon here wrote one of the best abbreviated examples of wisdom that exists. You see, wisdom is the big picture; it is the bird's-eye view. It is the twenty-year plan. Knowledge is the microscope plan; composed of short-term goals.

Activation

Wisdom takes self-reflection. There are no shortcuts to wisdom. Today I want you to think about a problem or situation that has troubled you, maybe for a long time. There is probably some level of emotion around it. It could be frustration or regret or anger. Set the emotion to the side. Write down the facts of the situation from your perspective, and then write the opposing view. Think about what is at stake. Can you find a compromise? What would a wise person do here to find peace or achieve extraordinary success?

Think ahead and make a wise plan. Use strategy and throw off the ways of impulse. Work your plan!

CHAPTER 3

Believe In Your Work

In 2018, my wife and I sold all we had, bought an RV, and took our four young children to live on the road. Everything we owned was on four wheels. When traveling through the north states of this great country, we stopped at the Battlefield of Little Bighorn in Montana.

The Battle was almost 150 years ago, and you may remember learning a bit about it in history class. The Great Sioux War was a significant loss to our nation on our 100th birthday, not what Congress was wanting to hear. 268 Soldiers died and 55 severely wounded.

It's recorded that Sitting Bull received spiritual insight about the battle and advised Chief Gall and Crazy Horse to fight valiantly, but afterwards not to touch the American's plunder. They heeded only the first advice.

The public reaction was mixed but Custer is largely remembered as an icon of the time because of the multiple battles he fought in as well as battlefield promotions he received.

It was amazing to stand where Custer and his men fell. I felt the ground where there was the chaos of the battlefield, something I have also experienced personally. Yelling of orders, screams of pain, the unspoken images as life flashes before eyes and one breathes his last breath. I could actually feel the ground speak to me in ways I hadn't experienced before.

It was there I looked out in the direction from where General Custer approached the Indians in ambush and thought, "how did he get ambushed? The terrain was on his side. His was the ambush element, yet he got ambushed."

Custer was a rising star in America's military and quickly rose through the ranks as he served in Lincoln's military. Custer aligned himself with the vision of fighting the South and freeing African Americans from the bondage of slavery. His tactic was simple brutality. He knew he was going somewhere and was one of the first generals to understand the power of the media. He continually employed photographers and journalists to follow him and record what he was doing. Today there's a plethora of images and articles that look further into his career. My belief is that he had long-term plans to run for the presidency.

After the Civil War, John Wilkes Booth took the life of an American president, but Custer was still at his post. The North and South were, in fact, exactly what Lincoln said they would be: "either one thing or the other." On the surface, we were one country united against owning other humans. The cause shifted into expanding our territory.

American settlers were purchasing land and pushing indigenous peoples west (or just away from where we wanted to live). General Custer was called on again to perform his duties as a soldier. He responded with his media entourage. Even though history books don't comment on it, I believe he didn't like this mission Congress had bestowed upon him.

HUNTING NATIVE AMERICANS WAS THE EXACT ANTITHESIS OF WHAT HE STOOD FOR IN THE CIVIL WAR. IT WAS EXACTLY OPPOSITE TO HIS PREVIOUS MISSION. HE WENT FROM FREEING A PEOPLE TO ENSLAVING A PEOPLE. Deep down, I believe Custer resented his task but was unable to voice his dissatisfaction. Like many men, he didn't know how to express his feelings, so he repressed them and drove onward like a good soldier does. Standing there, wondering how he lost, I believe that in the end, he didn't want the win as bad as the Indians did.

HIS MORAL BEARINGS FOR WANTING TO FREE PEO-PLE ARE COMMENDABLE, BUT AT THE SAME TIME, HIS LACK OF BELIEF IN HIS WORK SABOTAGED HIS COMMIT-MENT AND ENDED HIS LIFE.

Military Side

In BUD/S, we were taught about self-sabotage and self-pres-ervation. In the moment of a training routine, we would yell at one another, "What are you doing? You're sabotaging yourself!" What we learned was THAT IF YOU'RE NOT 100 PERCENT ALIGNED WITH WHAT YOU ARE DOING, YOU'RE GOING TO HOLD BACK FROM GIVING IT YOUR ALL AND SEEING A MAT-TER COMPLETED. If we have belief, we have no passion, and our efforts fail.

I also believe we all sabotage ourselves professionally in small ways every day. Remember being fourteen years old and being told to clean your room? Do you recall the lack of passion for the task at hand? Suddenly, in the face of tasks required, which we aren't fully aligned with, we develop stage 4 laziness, a sickness in need of doctoral care.

The reality is that you're not lazy. You're simply not aligned with the cause or don't believe in the mission. Are we really expected to wake up early and work hard every day for something we don't even care about? One of the best ways to sell something is to passionately believe in it.

Marketplace

In January of 2017, Bill Gates and Warren Buffett spoke at Columbia University. At the end of their talks, they opened the floor for Q and A with the audience. One person asked, "What's the next best field we should work in?" Mr. Buffett answered, "Don't worry about the next field, just do what you like and you'll succeed."

These very successful men, who began their empires with very few resources, understood the power of believing in their work and that chasing after the next big thing is unfulfilling and doesn't work.

A powerful motivator to follow your God-given dreams and talents.

Biblical Perspective

To the angel of the church in Pergamum write: These are the words of him who has the sharp, double-edged sword. I know where you live—where Satan has his throne. Yet you remain true to my name. You did not renounce your faith in me, not even in the days of Antipas, my faithful witness, who was put to death in your city—where Satan lives. Nevertheless, I have a few things against you: There are some among you who hold to the teaching of Balaam, who taught Balak to entice the Israelites to sin so that they ate food sacrificed to idols and committed sexual immorality. Likewise, you also have those who hold to the teaching of the Nicolaitans. Repent therefore! Otherwise, I will soon come to you and will fight against them with the sword of my mouth. Whoever has ears, let them hear what the Spirit says to the churches. To the one who is victorious, I will give some of the hidden manna. I will also give that person a white stone with a new name written on it, known only to the one who receives it. (Revelations 2:12–17)

This is an interesting verse in which a white stone is given to someone. There has been much debate about the idea around what might this stone represents but little clarity. Allow me to share what happened over ten years ago when I read this line, probably for the

7th or 8th time. This time, it suddenly leapt off the page at me and I had a realization. It's as if I had a veil in front of my eyes and then the veil was lifted and I understood. The understanding I got was the white stone represented a new name, but not just that; it was like an understanding of your new name. It represents a new calling and a new passion in life. The "born-again" experience followed by a deeper passion and fire.

You see, when you understand what you're made for, everything else melts away and you're left with a pursuit that grows as you pursue it.

I hope you're ignited with focusing on your God-given strength and stop with the in-between distractions.

Activation

Some of us have ticking time bombs in our culture, team fabric, and individual mindsets that we don't even know about. Being separated from our cause is one of them. Reflect on this and ask yourself if you are where you're supposed to be in terms of your career. Your subconscious will tell you immediately. Go with your initial answer and stop doing something you're not excited about. Or you may end up like Custer.

CHAPTER 4

Humility

Humility is not typically the first trait that comes to mind when you think about great business leaders like Steve Jobs, Jeff Bezos, Elon Musk, or Bill Gates.

Visionary, courageous, charismatic—these are the qualities most of us associate with great leaders. The idea of a humble self-effacing leader often doesn't resonate.

A number of research studies have concluded that humble leaders listen more effectively, inspire great teamwork, and focus everyone (including themselves) on organizational goals better than leaders who don't score high on humility.

I SUSPECT HUMILITY GETS A BAD RAP BECAUSE IT IS SOMETIMES LINKED WITH SUBSERVIENCE, WEAK-

NESS, OR INTROVERSION. And like everything else, this is a quality that needs to be developed.

When I travel to high schools or go to a venue where my audience is younger, I always encourage them to start their life with a good foundation regardless of their external circumstances. Good character and values will set people up for a promising future in many ways. The absence of character is like a time bomb ready to explode and wreck what they might set out to build.

These time bombs may look like verbal challenges from coworkers, frustration with your pay, dissatisfaction with your employees, resentment or holding onto offenses from people, gossiping about your competitors, pride in your abilities, judging someone, being enticed by other professionals to bend the rules, or by any number of frustrations.

These time bombs are all examples of things that can tear down what you've built. Not only do they have the ability to tear you down, but they also have the ability to build something in place of your success, a bad reputation. If you knew before starting something that this was probable, would you even start? WOULD YOU GET MARRIED IF YOU KNEW YOU'D GET DIVORCED? WOULD YOU START A BUSINESS IF YOU KNEW IN THE FUTURE

YOU'D HAVE TO DECLARE BANKRUPTCY? Don't you want to know how to avert disaster?

Military Side

When I was in Navy SEAL sniper school, we learned many things about what can affect the trajectory of a bullet. Wind, humidity, direction, elevation change, distance, ammunition, and length of barrel on the gun were all factors. Do you know the most important factor? Me.

I was the most important factor to my success. You see, my body was the biggest influencer of sending my bullet away. It was all in how I set up. It's very important, at times, to aim in a direction away from the target in order to hit the target. It's the same way in life. Sometimes we may have to avoid the lure of doing something quicker or cheaper, take the humble road, or pass on an opportunity to achieve our most important goal of a good reputation.

In training, I was taught to lay perfectly still, find my target in the sights, then shut my eyes and take a breath. If when I reopened my eyes, the target was not exactly where it was when I closed my eyes; something needed to be changed in my body's position so that I was aligned correctly. It wasn't the gun that needed to move; a small movement in me was needed. Maybe my elbow needed to be propped up. Maybe I needed to throw my leg three inches to the left. The eye test must set your crosshairs exactly on the target every time when shutting and reopening them.

WHILE LIVING LIFE AND CHASING DREAMS, WE HAVE GOALS, YES, BUT THE MOST IMPORTANT FACTOR IN HITTING GOALS IS HOW WE SET UP FOR THEM. PRACTICING GOOD CHARACTER, ESPECIALLY BEING HUMBLE, will always do us well.

Humility builds trust. George Macdonald said, "To be trusted is a better compliment than being loved."

In the Navy's best offensive task force, there is no place for pride. Pride is a killer. It leads to complacency. It creates laziness. It affects your attitude and makes others not want to work with you. YOU'LL LOSE OPPORTUNITIES BECAUSE OF Y-O-U. YOU'LL LOSE MONEY, CREDIBILITY, AND YOU'LL HAVE TO WORK FIVE TIMES HARDER TO MAKE THINGS WORK FOR YOU THAN IF YOU JUST EMPLOY HUMILITY IN AN AUTHENTIC FASHION.

Marketplace

In sports, coaches will usually favor an athlete who is coachable and respectful over a more talented athlete with a big ego.

I personally know a young man who was the number one high school wide receiver in Washington, Idaho, and Oregon states. He had great stats for touchdowns, interceptions, and punt returns. His highlight reel showed him making the defense look like they did not have legs.

Athletically, he had every reason to get a full-ride football scholarship to his choice of schools. But when colleges called his coach, he honestly told them, "Don't waste your time. He's full of himself and has a bad attitude."

Most of us have come across someone like this. Who do people prefer to associate with: someone who shares the road or the person who hogs it? Who do you think leaders want on their teams? An honest humble person or someone who believes they are smarter than everyone else?

Biblical Perspective

The good book has much to say about humility. In the book of Luke, Jesus tells a parable to teach us to avoid embarrassment.

> When someone invites you to a wedding feast, do not take the place of honor, for a person more distinguished than you may have been invited. If so, the host who invited both of you will come and say to you, "Give this person your seat." THEN, HUMILIATED, YOU WILL HAVE TO TAKE THE LEAST IMPORTANT PLACE. But when you are invited, take the lowest place, so that when your host comes, he will say to you, "Friend, move up to a better place." Then you will be honored in the presence of all the other guests. For all those who exalt themselves will be humbled, and those who humble themselves will be exalted. (Luke 14:8–11)
>
> Do nothing out of selfish ambition or vain conceit. Rather, in humility value others above yourselves. (Philippians 2:3)

A leader who follows the Lord can distinguish this principle and engrain it into their daily walk as an advantage to their leadership abilities.

I once had a conversation with a man about this very topic. His thoughts were reasonable, and he didn't like this principle. He said, "Where is the line as a Christian? Should we allow people to disrespect us and just take it as a pushover, or stand up for ourselves?"

MY REPLY WAS SIMPLE: "WHO IS GOD? YOU OR HIM?" YOU SEE, AT WHICH POINT WE JUSTIFY OURSELVES TO BE THE ONES TO FIGHT OUR BATTLES IS THE POINT THAT GOD STOPS FIGHTING ON OUR BEHALF.

Take for example the prophet Samuel in the Old Testament. The Bible says that God made it so that none of his words fell to the ground. Not him, God.

Paul understood this well when he said in 2 Timothy 4:14, "Alexander the metalworker did me a great deal of harm. The Lord will repay him for what he has done."

He knew that God would have his back and his real opposition wasn't' Alexander the copper worker, it was his own stubborn self-reliance inside of him.

So if we are looking to prop ourselves up and not God, then yes, we will have to pull every string we can to look pomp in front of people. But if we trust in God, he will be the one to establish us as a leader in the long run, influencing others in good ways. So our obedience to God's ways is required to receive God's blessing as a leader.

In reality, the choice is ours. We have the choice in doing the rooster march of dominance and pride around our groups to establish ourselves or not. The choice is and always will be yours personally. Yet if you choose to do it alone, in this matter, there is another Bible verse that may pertain to that decision.

> It will be as though a man fled from a lion only to meet a bear, as though he entered his house and rested his hand on the wall only to have a snake bite him. (Amos 5:19)

IT'S ALMOST LIKE AMOS IS TALKING ABOUT TRYING TO ESTABLISH OURSELVES IN OUR OWN POWER AND NOT THE LORD'S HUMILITY COULD BE LIKENED TO THE FLESHLY PURSUIT OF WRESTLING AND OVERPOWERING A LION OR BEAR. We get tired and out of breath from the dominance dance, only to be bitten by a situation that you do not know or understand. Lacking humility is a time bomb. One of which we do not see coming until it's too late. Yet another blind spot we all need to be humble enough to listen to others about.

Again, the choice is yours.

Activation

I'm not asking you if you yourself are humble. Of course, you'll say yes but would a truly humble man say yes? I want you to ask someone you see every day at work, someone who may not seem to like you: "Am I humble?" They may hesitate, but you'll get a full response. At the end of it, you'll also make a friend that respects and trusts you more. Mark my words, a future time bomb will have been diffused.

CHAPTER 5

Continuous Improvement

Win the battle before it even begins.

Many people love history. Historical events and stories can be educational. We can crawl inside each perspective and, sometimes, feel like we're in the event with all the characters.

There is an adage that says, 'history repeats itself.' WHY DOES IT REPEAT ITSELF? WELL, ONE OF THE REASONS HISTORY REPEATS ITSELF IS BECAUSE PEOPLE DON'T LEARN FROM THE PAST. You see, if General Custer died and we did not learn anything from it, his death was in vain. As strong of a statement that is, his death and all others' deaths are used by God for specific reasons, if we listen. Listen to the life they lived and judge it accordingly. It's important we honor their lives by remembering it and adding the good to our lives. Otherwise, history will repeat itself. That and there is a good chance that a lot of us that are living will suffer as well. Learning lessons from history is paramount because there are principles of character, golden nuggets, we can all add to our lives.

IF WE DON'T LEARN FROM HISTORY WE ARE ONLY LIKE THAT DISOBEDIENT YOUNG BOY WHO KEEPS GET-TING SPANKED FOR HIS ACTIONS, YET KEEPS DOING IT. This is the lesson of this chapter.

Reading books can be an important part of finding out who we are and who we should be. It's vital, especially when you plateau and think you're not advancing. Reading character building books like this one are a huge part of your advancing. In reality, you are positioning yourself, lining up your sights for the next level, when an opportunity intersects with your preparation for it.

Now follow me here and stretch your mind. Most people don't know the sister that history stories have: and that is…future stories. Your future stories are a mirror image across your present time com-pared to your past. YOU SEE, YOUR STUDY OF PAST EVENTS PREDICTS YOUR FUTURE. If you study and learn from it, it will prevent the same thing from happening in the future. If you are a busy body and don't take time to study it, you will most likely repeat it in the future.

Get it yet? Here's another example, just so the stragglers can catch up. Imagine a sheet of paper with three dots printed on it. One on the left, middle and right. The dot in the middle represents your current present time. Now fold the paper over. Hopefully the other two dots are touching and this represents sister events. They can be compared. Again, if you don't learn from your past, those sister events will look similar.

Ouch, right?

Now that the stragglers have caught up let's talk about people who study the past and people who study the future. Historians and prophets. YOU SEE, THERE'S REALLY LITTLE DIFFERENCE BETWEEN A HISTORIAN WHO UNDERSTANDS THE PAST AND A PROPHET WHO CAN FORETELL THE FUTURE. Most people relate to both types without knowing the real marriage these two professions have. A historian is one looking backward who is able to tell you what lessons you should know, and how to apply to the future.

A prophet looks forward and reveal how to apply the lessons from the past for what is coming.

Well, Charles, you say, "I don't believe in prophets foretelling the future." Well, my friend, do you watch the weather and prepare? Do you watch the stock market forecasts and prepare? Preparation never hurt anyone, and history lessons should be a big part of how you prepare for the future. OTHERWISE, YOU'RE LIKE A MAN WALKING WITH A BLINDFOLD DOWN THE STREET, SMILING AND WAVING AT PEOPLE WHILE YOU'RE BUMPING INTO POLES AND SIGNS. History lessons can prophesize your future.

But, Charles, you may say, history lessons are great and interesting and all, but times have changed, and this is a modern world. The lessons from long ago don't apply to today.

Let's take an example from the Alamo. The battle for Texas in 1836 would never have happened if the New Mexican President Santa Anna wasn't a centralist dictator. He set the standard for an umbrella Catholic religion and his states revolted.

If you take time and seek meaning from his legacy, I'd say we can apply it to parenting. Parents shouldn't act like dictators to their children as they turn into teenagers, or they risk revolt. Parents can take lessons from a Mexican president from two hundred years ago. An outdated principle? Not in the least.

Wayne Gretzky was a great hockey player. One day a journalist asked him the secret to his success. His answer made him famous: "I skate to where the puck is going to be, not where it is." Usually, his predictions were right, and he found himself in a place to make big plays.

We need to do the same in our professional leadership lives. Professionally go to where the business will be, not where it's at. Sometimes I watch the way culture ebbs and flows in the marketplace endeavors. It's a fast pace rat race that's constantly changing. In some cases, when you see other people going in one direction, you should go in another direction.

Marketplace

If you know where you want to go as a leader, you need to take advice from those who have already gone in that direction. One lesson you could learn from people who run companies is how to climb the corporate pyramid, not the corporate ladder. Climbing the ladder is what everyone else is doing, not what you should be fully focused on.

When I finished my service in the military, I didn't have a career plan. I used my GI Bill and enrolled in a local college's business course. There I was, a twenty-four-year-old ex-Navy SEAL trying to blend in as I figured out what all this college stuff was about.

To my surprise, I learned everything except what it takes to be in business. I didn't learn about persistence, character, manners, or how to sit with good posture and make eye contact during job interviews. Yet I did pick up a few nuggets around the campus that I used a decade or so down the road.

One day an older executive woman came to speak in my economics class about how to climb the corporate ladder. She explained that the goal was to eventually attain the top step: CEO. She expounded that to run a company you had to have a functional knowledge about how each department ran: marketing, production, HR, projections, sales, accounting, operations, and lobbying.

So, it's not exactly the corporate ladder; it's the corporate pyramid that should be sought after with zeal. Now if you're thinking, "How can I get a four-year degree to work in each of those departments?" don't worry, you don't need to. All you need to do is get your foot in the door with a company. You may or may not need a degree for that. Persistence while interviewing and a good attitude can be enough.

Once we get our foot in the door, we can apply lessons from history. While everyone else is trying to get a promotion going up, you know very well that any lateral position will help you more in ten years than climbing a single rung ladder. Take that lesson from history and put a request in for every position that pops open laterally in other departments. WITH A GOOD ATTITUDE AND LATERAL MOVEMENT, ONE DAY YOU'LL BE RUNNING THE SHOW.

I remember one day my wife and I were sitting with another couple talking about life. The wife was explaining how her husband should be running the company he worked for and how he was smarter than everyone else there. She became quite passionate, but the truth was the opposite of what her words were saying. He was young and full of ego as he came home and gossiped about the faults of those leading the company.

HE THOUGHT HE WAS SMART, HE REALLY DID. YET A PROMOTION WOULD HAVE ONLY REVEALED THAT HE HAD MORE FAULTS THAN THOSE HE WAS JUDGING. What he needed was to move around laterally in the company until he had a solid perspective of how the entire organization functioned. As soon as he had the experience necessary paired with a solid professional character, he would then be promotable to a leadership position.

Military Side

In the SEAL teams we had a saying to prepare for the future by accounting for something we learned in the past. It is the first tenant of Murphy's Law. Murphy's Law #1 states that whatever can break will break (mostly at the exact moment you need it), or sometimes it is referenced as anything that can go wrong will go wrong. SEALs COUNTER MURPHY'S LAW WITH A SAYING, "TWO IS ONE AND ONE IS NONE," WHICH TRANSLATES TO, MOST EVERYTHING YOU TRUST WILL BREAK AT JUST THE MOMENT YOU NEED IT—SO DOUBLE UP.

Preparing for Murphy's law looked like this: I was the comms guy in our platoon. My job was to carry the radio. The radio is called the biggest gun in the platoon because, with it, I could call down fire from the sky.

Now I didn't take two radios with me; they are about twenty pounds each. I did, however, carry extra antennae, batteries, and mouthpieces though.

A three-day mission would go through a set of batteries each day. I carried a second set "just in case." Add to that ammo, water, food, my gun, med kit, camera equipment, and it made for a heavy pack and long days on the side of a mountain.

One of the instructors from BUD/S training tried to explain to us a time when good old Uncle Murphy came and paid his unit a visit during an op. He told us of a hard lesson they learned setting up an ambush one night in Asia. His platoon was called in to stop a group of rebels that had been robbing businesses in the province and growing in strength. They did their research and learned that the rebel convoy would be coming through a mountain road. They chose a choke point and set up an ambush. His job was to use his automatic weapon and take out the front vehicle. That was also to signal the rest of the platoon to engage in their different parts of the ambush.

He explained that as he saw the headlights coming down the road how nervous he became. When it came time, he rammed the trigger to the back of the trigger housing compartment to light up the first vehicle. His fully automatic weapon only fired one shot. For whatever reason, his gun just misfired.

He racked the weapon, put the vehicle in his sights, and rammed the trigger to the back of the housing again. Bang, one round went off and then nothing. He had just given away their position and he still didn't know why his gun was malfunctioning. His platoon also was curious as to why they didn't hear the roaring of his gun to signal everything else.

The confusion and chaos of the battlefield set in. He ended up having to individually rack and fire every single round. A rate of about 10 bullets per second. He should've had 150 rounds through that gun in less than 15 seconds. Later he found out that some of the components in his automatic weapon had gotten worn out, so it went from automatic function to semiautomatic. At the very moment he needed it, Murphy's law showed up loud and proud.

Just like the best and the proudest know in the military, some things are in your control while other things are not. You cannot have what you want all the time, but you can set yourself up for success. Like the great Wayne Gretzky said, "I skate to where the puck is going. to be, not to where it has been."

Another example of this happened while serving Uncle Sam. I was eager to get all the training and qualifications as was possible. I was able to take a civilian interview course and pick up training in the Arabic language. With both these qualifications in my arsenal I was a top candidate to attend an interrogation course put on by the FBI. This class was important as it is something that can really extend the scope of jobs for a soldier once out of the military.

The FBI course would have opened many doors for me both in and out of the service. I applied for it, and it was looking like a thumbs-up for approval based on my current qualifications in both language and interrogating. After a few days, my CO (commanding officer) called me in. A rare thing to happen with the younger "team guys" like me. He wanted to personally tell me why he had just denied my application.

Although qualified, he explained I wasn't able to take the FBI interrogation course because I didn't have any gray hair. I remember saying to myself, "Excuse me, what does that mean?" I was confused. What had that to do with my ability to learn about some of the best methods of interrogation.

He explained that if I were to fill that role while on deployment, I wouldn't be successful at eliciting information from our enemy. Arab culture was different from ours. He said that "when you enter the room and you don't have gray hair, the men won't feel as if they need to answer to you or respect you." It's a cultural barrier and my CO went on to choose someone older who had some gray hair growing in as it could command the respect of people when he entered the room.

My CO knew something about history and was able to prepare his team for success.

Biblical Perspective

Joseph was a man of continuous improvement. He was thrown in a pit, sold to traders, made to work, thrown in jail again, but then after twenty-two years or so was promoted to the greatest position in the land. You see, he took advantage of every opportunity to prepare for the next.

When he was betrayed and sold into slavery at a young age, he used that opportunity and learned to trust God.

When he worked for Potiphar, in his household, he used that period of his life to learn to read and write the Egyptian language, mathematics, and management skills.

When Joseph was thrown in jail, he used that time to learn how to interpret dreams.

When he was reunited with his family, he learned how to forgive.

You see, every setback for Joseph was used to get ready for what came next. He didn't get upset with the short-term happenings; he kept his eye on the long-term and leveraged even things that seemed to be setbacks to work in his favor. I almost feel somewhat like a prosperity preacher saying these things right now, but it's true. You see, God prepares his children for higher causes by giving them difficulties so they can grow their character as necessary, if they would allow it. Joseph did this. In fact, he named his firstborn son, Manasseh, which meant, "God has made me forget all my trouble."

CONTINUING SELF-IMPROVEMENT AND LEARNING FROM HISTORY ARE VITAL PARTS FOR US TO BECOME

WISE AND REPUTABLE LEADERS. I want to encourage you to make self-development an important part of your life and to learn from history. Look within yourself to find your Custer moment and learn from the mistakes of others. Don't believe the lie that your plateau will last forever. With the right preparation, anything is possible. Use the past to align yourself with the future and prepare for success. After all, that's what a leader does.

Hopefully, as a leader, you'll use each and every character nugget possible to achieve the next level. As they say, "Another level, another devil."

Activation

Today I want you to strike up a conversation with someone older, at least eighty years old. You may have to go to a senior living establishment and sit in the lobby for a while. This is in stark contrast to gaining wisdom from some kind of continuing education curriculum.

You see, programs are marketed and designed for you to purchase, but may not necessarily help you. These programs will tell you what they want you to know; but someone from the previous generation will tell you what you need to know. Maybe bring some milk and cookies and offer them to anyone who will speak with you as it is good to show gratitude for what you will learn. Ask questions. Then keep your lips together (listen).

Ask them how they achieved it and what mistakes they made. THE AGED HAVE A WEALTH OF KNOWLEDGE AND THEY LOVE THE INTERACTION. Since they don't care about being professional anymore, they will simplify and dumb things down for you while putting it bluntly. What do they have to lose ?

I think we may have just had a miscommunication. My intuitions are telling me to talk you into today's activation a little bit more. Listen, I know this is a bit abstract. Did you just justify a reason not to go? I know, I know. You're doing this thing, or you have to go to that place. Well, today cancel it and go find an elderly person to sit with. Your ability to do this actually launches you farther than you know toward being a good leader, and in more ways than one.

Did you just make another excuse to blow off this activation? Don't have time? Listen, you don't have time not to. Before the sun goes down tonight, fight, tear, strain, and bleed to seek wisdom from someone who has lived it. Three, two, one, go.

CHAPTER 6

Embody Endurance

You know that feeling you get when your alarm clock first wakes you up in the morning? "Can I skip my commitments and sleep in a little bit more?" You may hit the snooze button. Some of us pop right up. That right there is what separates those who make it big and those who almost make it big. The thought to push things off for "later" is laziness. Laziness in all forms kills your ability to achieve more and build momentum. YOU CAN HAVE ALL THE OTHER QUALIFICATIONS OF A LEADER AND LACK THE MOST IMPORTANT ONE: ENDURANCE.

Endurance, and its twin sister, spontaneous endurance, are the opposites of laziness. Having just a hint of laziness is a time bomb for someone espousing to be a good leader. An "I'll do it later" attitude can cause corrosion in productivity with a reputation that follows. You'll miss out on so many things that eat up your margins. A few meetings here and a few contracts there will slip through the cracks. A missed opportunity or slower production can make you the point of bottleneck in your company.

A person can be lazy because that is our natural state of tendency when born. We are all born with it. Some people are ok with making slothyness a part of their personality and being. But I believe that if you want to be a leader, you must learn how to get your mind off of yourself and on to the opportunity you have to serve others with constant and extreme excitement.

Military Side

In the SEALS, we have a central part in BUD's training that everyone is well aware of. The Bell. Since Special Warfare training is voluntary at all times, your allowed to leave at any moment. It's really a test of someone's mental psychology when you allow them to choose to endure the beating. If you've never heard of it before, the bell is what you ring 3 times to signify to the rest of your BUD's class that you quit. It is a shiny object the instructor staff keeps you well aware of at all times. IN A BRIEF MOMENT OF WEAK-

NESS AND DESPAIR, YOU CAN END YOUR DISCOMFORT

AND LEAVE TRAINING.

In SEAL training the saying goes, "If the quitting bell was right next to your bedside, no one would make it through training." I still remember waking up to my alarm clock. In big red digital numbers, it said, "3:20 a.m." There was no such thing as hitting the snooze button during training. It was "jump up," and the going didn't end until well after the sun went down. Some of us had only gone to bed a few hours earlier. If you didn't prepare your gear for the next day the night before, you would fail miserably as if your day wasn't already hard enough.

A few of those early mornings started on the beach. I remember standing on the beach of Coronado Island. The ocean was roaring. It was at least a quarter-mile long surf zone with waves reaching eight to ten feet high at times. In much of our training, we geared up and swam all the way out while maintaining an arm's length distance from our swim buddy. Then we'd do it again to practice for that one mission we call our bread and butter, or "Over the Beach." When there is no way in and our military needs to gain access into a nation, we take the beaches. It's the reason JFK birthed the SEAL teams in 1962. We would spend hours rehearsing just that.

The tactic for swimming through the waves to the end of the surf zone to get out past the waves is one that requires endurance, to say the least. A swimmer must aggressively dive underneath the waves as they go over you. The bigger the wave, the deeper you need to go under it. Sometimes it took my swim buddy and me forty-five minutes to complete the sole task of swimming past the breakers to calm water. There were times when we would dive under a big wave and come up for a gasp of air but realize there was another wave stacked right behind it, unseen to someone who only has the vantage point of their head bobbing in the water.

Have you ever tried to take a much-needed breath of air while swimming and all you got was a big gulp of water? It catapults the panic reaction straight to the core of your brain and all you can do is think about getting above the water. We would do that only to find ourselves facing another wave, ready to get pushed back under again, and the cycle continues to spiral down from there.

In SEAL training, there is no quit. Whether you get up early or push yourself to the limits battling through monster waves, endurance is the component that gets you to completion. You don't turn around. You don't stop what you're doing because it gets difficult. You push forward to complete the task.

In the example of swimming through the surf zone, this training was for a real-world-mission, and you weren't going to give up. Jumping on an extract platform out at sea is all we were able to do sometimes. GIVING IN TO THE CRUSHING OF THE WAVES WOULD MEAN BEING PUSHED BACK INTO SHORE WHERE THE ENEMY LIVES. AGAIN, IN A REAL-WORLD MISSION, THAT OPTION IS NOT AN OPTION.

It takes the utmost endurance of the mind and body, trying to emerge as a leader in the marketplace. Sometimes it's like swimming through a long surf zone because wave after wave of trials and hardships end up staring you in the eyes every day. It is fully a mental decision—choosing what your best option is—not a physical ability to make most of your required decisions.

SOMETIMES YOU WANT TO THROW OUT YOUR PROFESSIONAL CHARACTER AND FREAK OUT ON THE WORLD. YOU CAN'T. THE PRESSURE CAN GET SO GREAT, YOU FEEL LIKE YOU'RE LOSING YOUR MIND AT THE EXACT MOMENT YOU SHOULD NOT. I want to encourage you to keep going and forge along, building a good reputation, and don't give in to people pulling you into traps that would tarnish your reputation.

Hopefully, you have gathered that endurance in the market-place is a great lesson learned from the successful military battles and training requirements. But in the marketplace, you keep your aim through all the intangible barriers and hurdles that try to pull you down as you reach for higher goals.

Marketplace

Let's examine endurance by viewing some of the main princi-ples other leadership authors have written about. Let's see what they say. There have been many studies about the different characteristics successful people have. A quick study of these characteristics should give us a glimpse of what other teachers and coaches say in the field.

Michael Jordan was cut from his high school basketball team—a heartbreaking experience for any teenager.

J. K. Rowling had her first Harry Potter novel rejected twelve times and was told "not to quit her day job."

Stephen King's first book, *Carrie*, accumulated at least thirty rejec-tion slips before it was accepted by Doubleday.

Legend has it that *Jack London's* first story was rejected six hun-dred times before finally being published.

Oprah Winfrey's on-air career had a rocky start. She was hired as co-anchor of the evening news at Baltimore's ABC affiliate, an enviable job for a young journalist, but was dropped after just a few months. She was sent from the anchor chair to an assortment of less prestigious jobs, including writing and street reporting.

What similar themes do you see in all these people? It's endurance. It's what separates those who make it big from those who almost make it big. This is how. Every person mentioned above stuck to their guns. They did not give in. They were not guaranteed wealth or fame; they were simply determined to stick to their chosen path.

Listen, I've spent a lot of time on the edge of hypothermia training with the SEALs yet quitting never occurred to me. All I could think about was the task at hand. I've also spent time in the hottest climate on earth. Same thing. **I NEVER THOUGHT ABOUT QUITTING, JUST ABOUT THE TASK AT HAND.**

When I left the SEALs, I worked several other jobs. For over two years, I worked as personal security for one of the wealthiest men on the planet. But it was not what I really wanted to do.

I left that position and opened a CrossFit gym. I started in my garage, and at first, it was slow going. I took a risk and moved into a warehouse space down the road. I was not making much money after all my expenses and things were looking gloomy.

One day, while vacuuming the immense rubber mats that covered the floor of the entire gym, I received a phone call. It was a member who said he didn't want to belong to my gym anymore because we didn't have a lot of equipment. In response I did what I learned in the scriptures to bless and not curse, so I blessed him and thanked him for the time he did give us. Then, I stopped vacuuming. "What," I asked myself, "am I doing?" No one seems to notice, let alone appreciate how I am busting my butt, I'm spending every day away from my family, putting in long hours. "What am I doing?"

It was a moment of crisis. I had a choice to make. I looked around; it would be easy to leave the job of a business owner and go back to the security job. But a voice in my head said, "No." It was the same voice that pushed me through SEAL training, the same voice that kept my head on the nights in Iraq when carrying out the cause of Operation Iraqi Freedom.

This gym was my mission, and I was not quitting. I decided in that moment I would serve people in fitness with gladness and joy no matter if they appreciated it or not. Over the next seven years, I built up the revenue by serving my customers well. I worked harder rather than walk away. I sold it and I made some money—not like Stephen King or J. K. Rowling—but it's not about the money. It's about respecting people and following through.

Biblical Perspective

There is a Bible story I always wondered about. In the Old Testament, when God whittled down the army of Gideon (who was a scrawny weak dude) to almost nothing. I never really understood it until I really started praying and meditating on the story. All of a sudden, it came to me.

Gideon started with thirty-two thousand fighting men to deliver Israel out of the hands of the Midianites. The Midianites were so oppressive to the Israelites that they had to live in the mountain clefts and caves. Whenever they planted crops, the Midianites would ruin their crops and kill their livestock. So as Gideon assembled the army, God said, "You have too many men. Get rid of the ones who tremble with fear." That day, twenty-two thousand soldiers left. Next, God still insisted there were too many men.

You might ask, "How can you have too many men when fighting?" Well, if you ask that, you're not taking in this story. This story is about virtue and character. The next instructions were from Judges 7:5–7:

> So Gideon took the men down to the water.
> There the Lord told him, "Separate those who lap
> the water with their tongues as a dog laps from

those who kneel down to drink." Three hundred of them drank from cupped hands, lapping like dogs. All the rest got down on their knees to drink. The Lord said to Gideon, "with the three hundred men that lapped I will save you and give the Midianites into your hands. Let all the other men go home."

With that, Gideon had three hundred men to fight an entire army with. You might be asking as I was: "What does the way you drink water have to do with being able to fight?"

One group brought the water to their mouth; the other group brought their mouth down to the water, and that was the distinction. WHEN BRINGING WATER UP TO YOUR MOUTH, YOU'RE ALSO ABLE TO BE AWARE OF YOUR SURROUNDINGS; YOU'RE READY FOR ANYTHING. YOUR ENDURANCE IS UP; YOU'RE ACTIVATED. As I would tell my players when I coached basketball, "You're not allowed to rest by putting your hands on your knees and bending over." Doing so tells the other team that you're ready and waiting to be killed. The same applies to the ones God chose to serve in Gideon's army. The ones who took the lazy position were not fit to serve Gideon's kind of army.

The three hundred fighting men of Gideon were without fear and had ample endurance. They attacked the Midianites during the dark hours and chased them miles and miles across the countryside, winning a big victory.

There's one question I like to ask people when they are faced with a major decision: When it comes to times of endurance, what would the you from ten years from this moment tell the you now? I'm sure your future you would want the today you to put them in a better position. Honorable mention: key verses about endurance.

How long will you lie there, you sluggard?
When will you get up from your sleep? A little
sleep, a little slumber, a little folding of the hands
to rest—and poverty will come on you like a thief
and scarcity like an armed man. (Proverbs 6:9–11)

Through laziness, the rafters sag; because of
idle hands, the house leaks. (Ecclesiastes 10:18)

Activation

Take a moment. Think about Michael Jordan and the others. They became the best in their field of all time. What if the first failure had stopped them?

Now journal about where your life intersects with endurance. Who you see yourself being in five years? A leader who pushed through the hard times or someone who is off chasing another thing because it was easier? Think about it today; sleep on it tonight. How can you embody what you just wrote down? Then think: what is the one thing I can do today to make these journal pages come true? You just wrote your marching orders.

CHAPTER 7

Use Time as a Tool

I remember sitting as an eighteen-year-old sailor fresh out of boot camp, sitting in a finance class to get training in how to steward my money. All new sailors are required to attend this class. For some it's the first real exposure to a solid income and the military is trying to prevent their members from making bad decisions. A part of the class was about investing in funds that offer compounding interest. This was a new term for me, compounding interest, that opened up a new way of thinking about money.

I'm sure you know that compounding interest applies to money over your lifetime. I want to talk to you about how a leader can do the same thing not only with money, but also by leveraging time and patience in other aspects of your life. SEASONED LEADERS USE TIME AS A TOOL. IN FACT, IF A LEADER DOESN'T

UNDERSTAND AND APPLY THIS PRINCIPLE, HE OR SHE ISN'T THE BEST LEADER THEY CAN BE. That may sound steep and deep, but in this classroom of life, sometimes you need to shoot straight. If money can be compounded over a length of time, leaders need to learn what else they can compound with time.

Leveraging time is the one aspect that should give you overwhelming confidence that your endeavors will grow with success. That is as long as you don't plant any time bombs in your future.

I suggest that other than money, your reputation is one thing that can grow with compounding interest. A good name and a good reputation are also something that people fail to understand when leveraging time. Building a good reputation is often a less taught part of business, yet it can open more doors than a person's résumé can.

For example: Let's say you want to make a good reputation for yourself of being peaceful and nonconfrontational. Let's say that the neighboring business to you doesn't care about their reputation and they are rude every time they see you. What do you do? You can stoop down to their level and react to them the same way they treat you. But doing so means you're not building a peaceful and nonconfrontational reputation that can build interest over time the same way money compounds.

Choosing to be a reputable person means you have decided to act that way, and no one else can change that. In the example above, let's say for three years you don't react to your neighbor's insults and pestering. All it takes is one retaliatory act, and the reputation you're trying to build gets blown up, reset back to zero and voided.

"GIVING IN TO THE TUG OF PEOPLE AGAINST YOU IS WHAT WANNABE LEADERS DO, NOT WHAT ACTUAL LEADERS DO. BUILDING A REPUTATION IS DIFFICULT, BUT IF YOU KNOW WHAT YOU'RE DOING, IT'S INTENTIONAL AND EASY.

You see, if you only make nearsighted decisions based on what's profitable in the next few days, weeks, or months, your professional reputation will never come into bloom. Just like your retirement fund, it will never build to something that leaves a legacy. If you make decisions based on what's quick and easy in the present, a legacy may elude you.

Without using time as leverage, a person's normal workday will most likely resemble a pinball game (tell me you remember pinball!), bouncing off of people's reactions to them. What it should look like is a nice day out on the boat in calm weather. You should anticipate the same for tomorrow.

There must come a day when you decide you'd like to use time and play the long game in life. Once you're ready to stop going for low-hanging fruit day-to-day and reacting to outside forces upon your life, you're ready to excel at a fast rate. We all know and realize the power of compounding interest when applied to money. Consider applying it to these other categories as well for you to leverage:

1. Faith

2. Marriage

3. Parenting

4. Education

5. Fitness

6. Friendships

7. Character development

What would it look like to make a steady investment into those areas of your life similar to someone investing money into a 401k? With daily, weekly, and monthly care, investing in each category will help you gain in all areas. Hopefully you choose a good direction to mark your goal.

There are three possibilities for each category. First, a good investment that allows overflow. Second, a zero investment or negligence that yields a zero gain. Lastly, there is an incorrect investment that yields a reverse return.

Realize there is a great possibility for each area to <u>overflow</u> into the other areas with <u>good investing</u>. Wise incremental stewardship of these areas will yield an exponential return on investment. Exponential because a good measure of these areas will pour over into other areas. For example, steady parental investment will grow happy, confident, and mature children. This overflow happens when one day they will help you with your causes and business. One category spills over into another one. Character development spills over into the rest. Education spills over into the rest. Keep in mind that good investing spills over into the rest along with negative investing. For example, neglect spills over into the rest.

Military Side

In the SEAL teams, everyone there has something in common. We all know we are training to be the absolute best. When training is completed, we know we are all a part of something special. Something different than the rest, I mean, what other training out there requires people to practically drown themselves? Uncle Sam gives us every tool necessary for success. This is the true secret to our success as a special warfare unit. We are given assets to get in and get out, tools and technology better than the rest of the world to help us while on the ground. No expense is spared when we are told to "go and do." We then take those tools and apply them to the battlefield as we best see fit. It's an investment principle that you can apply to your personal and professional life. The military has a group of guys who have invested in themselves; now the military is going to invest in them with more. Grab this idea. To whom much is given, much is required. (Luke 12:48)

Out of the above list of seven investment categories I've listed, do you know which area of investment affects all six others? Think about it. What category can increase the investment of all the other categories? Well, logically these categories can't unless the amount of time invested in each is longer. I would suggest that the fitness category can do that. It's the only one that can lengthen the amount of time you have on earth. THE LONGER YOU LIVE, THE LONGER YOU CAN INVEST, THE MORE COMPOUNDING CAN HAPPEN.

I would suggest that the more time and good investment you apply to these areas, the more return you get. This is why I challenge young men to put down the video game controller. It yields a below zero return in all areas because they invest vast amounts of time into something that will never return to them.

What happens when you don't apply any investment or just flat-out neglect one of these areas? This ultimately gives you a negative return in the category.

If one of these areas in your life doesn't yield a positive return, then it will suck away from the other areas. Think about it. If you put money into a savings account without getting any interest on it, is that a zero-balance investment? No, it's a negative investment because money is always losing value. If I saved $30,000 fifty years ago, I would have $30,000 today. Would that be a zero return? No, it would be a negative return if you factor in inflation.

Not only is there a zero return that can be assumed to be a negative return, but you lost all the time to use and leverage as well. It's all about how you use time.

We can talk with so much certainty and knowledge about money, but it applies equally to all other areas as well. This is what it looks like to have one of these areas negatively impact the other categories. Let's assume you don't give your marriage the proper investment needed to survive. Well, a divorce is costly and affects your financial status. In fact, it's been said there's nothing more financially draining than divorce and giving your ex-spouse half of your retirement. Painful, yes, but right or wrong?

I recently met a dentist who was very successful. He invested a lot of time into his professional career, but his marriage and parenting were lacking any substantial investment. After his kids graduated high school, he and his spouse divorced. He had to liquidate half of his assets and give them to his spouse. Now as a retired man, he lives on a chunk of savings and a Social Security check month-to-month. In his case, all the investment he made into his professional career and thinking that he was getting ahead by making money ended up 50 percent of what he thought it would be, and he also lost an entire category of investment (marriage) in the end. You see, if he would have made steady investments into his marriage, he would have been able to keep the assets he worked and invested so much in.

Hopefully I'm showing you this correctly and your realizing how the different areas of investment affect each other. Consider a negative way to invest in the category of fitness for example. When weightlifting, it's important to use the right form. Well, as much as possible. If you've lifted weights, you know that using the right form is more difficult. So the saying goes that if you 'get strong doing it wrong', your body is going to grow in a disproportionate and unbalanced fashion. If you take a little chip out of your ego and do less weight, you won't hurt yourself and you will get strong doing it right and that's when real longevity is forged. You see, investment isn't good if it's incorrectly invested. Would you invest in a stock that's going down? How about your job, your character development, or your faith?

A bad <u>investment can</u> yield negative interest. Don't make the mistake that you're investing in your marriage if you take your wife to the movies. That's just sitting in front of a screen without a lot of interaction.

THE SAME GOES WITH PARENTING YOUR CHILDREN. IF YOU NEGLECT PROPER AND REGULAR INVESTMENT NEEDED TO PRODUCE A PERSON CAPABLE OF ADDING VALUE TO SOCIETY, IT WILL AFFECT YOUR WALLET. You see it all the time. Kids living under their parents' roof decades past eighteen years old. They aren't adding value; they are taking away from you. Don't think that you're correctly investing in your children by being in the house with them at the same time. That's like having money in the bank at 0 percent interest. You must make eye contact with them and ask them difficult life questions to create conversations. Each of these categories of investment can take away from all the others.

Marketplace

Now to show you the real value in using time as leverage. It takes an internal character in your gut so strong you can withstand many storms.

There are many ways to examine leaders under pressure. The stock market is a good test. Someone who plays the stock market has to weather the price going up and the price going down. As prices go down, there's constantly the fear of losing more money. No one knows where the bottom of the stock price is going to be, so the temptation is to sell. It's a scary process and many people have lost money because they don't have a deeper grit and patience. Holding out over a long period shows strength. It shows commitment. It shows resolve. It shows a strong leader.

Please see that weathering the storms shows a strength of self and you're confident that when the dust settles you will triumph spectacularly. Might I add that this internal strength is the one reason people also make lots of money on the stock market?

The reason Warren Buffett has done so well in the stock market is that when the stocks go down and everybody is selling, he is buying. When the stocks go up and everybody is buying, he is selling.

He has a strong gut and I want you to develop the same for all the categories of investing.

Biblical Perspective

> The kingdom of heaven is like a mustard seed, which a man took and planted in his field. Though it is the smallest of all seeds, yet when it grows, it is the largest of garden plants and becomes a tree, so that the birds come and perch in its branches. (Matthew 13:30–32)

This shows God's investment strategy for investing in the area of faith. Little investments can grow something into an area of overflow. A seed grows into a tree that houses the birds. How much more would God allow a steady increase with steady investment to overflow in your life?

In fact, one day someone asked Martin Luther (the 1517 guy) a simple question: "If you knew you were to die tomorrow, what would you do today?"

He answered, "Even if I knew that tomorrow the world would go to pieces, I would still plant my apple tree."

A man like that understands how things work in this world. A man like that can be used by God to accomplish big things. In fact, he was used to do big things by writing his *95 Theses* and will be remembered for all of history.

You can apply this same resolve and commitment to all the other categories. Not the technical strategy used in the stock market, but the confidence in yourself that you're playing the right game and you're using time as a leverage tool for your success, and you stick out the storms to impact the world for a greater cause, get rich, and leave a legacy for yourself—a legacy that others will remember when you're gone. They'll say about you, "He/she had a way of never giving up," all because you stepped outside of time.

Activation

"Time" for you to break out the calendar. That's right, the old-fashioned kind with paper pages and days and dates filled in. I want you to write out the time you are going to invest before and after work in each of the eight categories.

This activation has three parts. I want you to go through each category and figure out how to make a good investment, a zero investment, and an incorrect investment. Be thorough and allow time for self-reflection. Here's a starter chart with some hints.

	Good Investment	Zero Investment	Incorrect Investment
Faith		No attention	
Marriage			
Money		Spend what you make.	Buy a bad stock.
Parenting			
Job/ Business	Bringing in a teamwork specialist.		Showing up late and unprepared.
Education			Seeking education without using it.
Fitness	Eating vegetables		Bad form when weightlifting. Eating sugar.
Friendships			Talking too much
Character Dev.		No external reading	

CHAPTER 8

Use Your Weirdness

When you think of Michael Jordan, what's the first thing that pops into your head? A red Chicago Bulls uniform flying through the air from the foul line? A bald head? Those things are true, but what about his tongue? His tongue? That's right, his tongue. His tongue would nearly drop to the floor as he was about to break down his defender. Don't believe me? Do an internet image search and see the truth of it.

Opponents, teammates and fans knew to watch out for it because when they saw it, they knew he was about to unglue the defense's feet and make them look like schoolyard kids. This small trait (followed by the annihilation of his opponent) distinguished him. It set him apart from the rest of the NBA. If you look at many notoriously famous leaders, they all have something unique the public finds entertaining or embarrassing.

- Tiger Woods has his fist bump uppercut.
- Barack Obama has those wide ears and slowly processed words.
- Virgin Airlines founder Richard Branson has the goatee and frosted hair.
- CNN host Anderson Cooper has the straight haircut and straight gaze.
- George Bush had the unique laugh and stiff gestures.

Each of those people have an aspect or trait that could be considered weird or awkward. But they are remembered for it.

Often in today's world, people don't want to let their weirdness be seen. I ask you to reconsider hiding yours and start using it. HERE'S THE DEAL. YOU HAVE A TRAIT THAT YOU CAN'T CHANGE. IT'S NOT SOMETHING TO HIDE; IT'S SOMETHING TO USE. IT'S INSPIRING TO SEE SOMEONE ALLOW THEMSELVES TO BE SEEN, AND IT BUILDS TRUST IN OTHERS.

That weird thing isn't going to hurt you unless you let it. Imagine if you will, a wave in the ocean. Each wave is different, none are the same. Could you imagine swimming out to waist-deep water and trying to stop the wave from reaching the shore?

Well, some people try to do this with their unique traits. Some people try to stop them. I would suggest that instead of trying to stop the wave, ride the wave. It will carry you to where you need to go.

This is what many successful people have figured out how to do. They didn't try to change themselves; they used their uniqueness to ride a wave to success.

Market Side

Have you ever heard of Alfred Matthew Yankovic? He sold over twelve million record albums and was one of the early stars on MTV. He earned five Grammy awards and a further eleven nominations, four gold records, and six platinum records in the United States. He even had his own television series. His preferred instrument was the accordion.

You might know him by his other name: Weird Al. His career began when a door-to-door salesman traveling through Lynwood offered the Yankovic parents a choice of accordion or guitar lessons at a local music school. Yankovic claims the reason his parents chose accordion over guitar was they were convinced it would revolution-ize rock.

The accordion went nowhere in the world of rock, but Weird Al did—by playing to his weirdness.

Military Side

Do you know how a firefight is won? You don't? I can't believe you wouldn't know that. Weird. Well, I'll tell you. It's not with metal flying through the air. It's not even by hitting and eliminating your target and enemy. It's through sound.

That's right, sound. When in a firefight with an enemy, the human tendency when being shot at is to seek cover and stay safe. Staying safe usually means to keep your head down. But if you're the one doing that, it will only restrict your team from successfully looking around and moving where they need to.

In the Teams, we train long hard hours specifically about how to move cohesively and fluidly as a team during a firefight in order to win firefights. Our team leaders call the shots and it's import-ant to listen because anything can change at any second. The battle-field is complete chaos. It's confusing and any singular person has only a fraction of information about the collective reality at any one moment. And as a team, it is the collective reality which is the focus. You can see why keeping your head up is important.

While engaging and moving toward or away from the enemy, it's imperative to maintain the sound of bullets being shot from our side toward their side at every second. THE SOUND OF A CONSISTENT BARRAGE OF BULLETS OVER THEIR HEADS KEEP THEM DOWN AND KEEPS THEM FROM SEEING THE BATTLE DEVELOP. NEVER SHOULD THERE BE A LULL IN THE AIR. NEVER SHOULD THERE BE SILENCE.

Keeping the enemies' heads down because they constantly hear bullets zinging past them allows us to move more securely. That's the trick. At any one point, if one of our team members hears silence for more than a second, everyone stops and lights up whoever is downrange. It makes a sixteen-man platoon the enemy just picked a fight with sound like a thousand-man army.

Just like using sound to help win a firefight, using your weirdness is another way for you to win. BEING YOURSELF IS LIKE SENDING A CONSTANT BARRAGE OF CONFIDENCE DOWNRANGE AT ANYONE WHO WANTS TO GO AGAINST YOUR CONFIDENCE AS A LEADER.

As you are seeking ways to gather a following, improve self-development, and impact the world, don't fight yourself and cover your flaws. They are not flaws; they are your reality. Don't waste your time trying to be someone other than who you are. Make sure people can trust you are who you say you are. Use it!

Biblical Perspective

The following passage was written by the prophet Isaiah about Jesus Christ the Messiah nearly seven hundred years or seventeen generations before Jesus was born. Some people like to ask me to prove God, so here you go, a prophecy describing him hundreds of years before his birth. As you read this prophecy about Jesus, you're going to notice your heart open up and your energy level raise. Happens every time. Also note that he had a trait that's not talked about much.

> *Who has believed our message and to whom has the arm of the Lord been revealed? He grew up before him like a tender shoot and like a root out of dry ground. He had no beauty or majesty to attract us to him, nothing in his appearance that we should desire him. He was despised and rejected by mankind, a man of suffering,*

and familiar with pain. Like one from whom people hide their faces he was despised, and we held him in low esteem. Surely, he took up our pain and bore our suffering, yet we considered him punished by God, stricken by him, and afflicted. But he was pierced for our transgressions, he was crushed for our iniquities; the punishment that brought us peace was on him, and by his wounds we are healed. He was oppressed and afflicted, yet he did not open his mouth, he was led like a lamb to the slaughter, and as a sheep before its shearers is silent, so he did not open his mouth. By oppression and judgment, he was taken away. Yet who of his generation protested? For he was cut off from the land of the living; for the transgression of my people, he was punished. He was assigned a grave with the wicked, and with the rich in his death, though he had done no violence, nor was any deceit in his mouth. Yet it was the Lord's will to crush him and cause him to suffer, and though the Lord makes his life an offering for sin, he will see his offspring and prolong his days, and the will of the Lord will prosper in his hand. After he has suffered, he will see the light of life and be satisfied; by his knowledge my righteous servant will justify many, and he will bear

their iniquities. Therefore, I will give him a portion among
the great, and he will divide the spoils with the strong,
because he poured out his life unto death, and was num-
bered with the transgressors. For he bore the sin of many
and made intercession for the transgressors. (Isaiah 53)

The piece to notice about Jesus from Isaiah is in verse 2 where it says, "no beauty or majesty to attract us to him, nothing in his appearance that we should desire him." I know this goes against popular thinking because there have seen many pieces of art that depict Jesus Christ as a man who is handsome, yet this verse says that's not so. To think that the number-one most popular person in all of history was described as not being attractive, as possessing no physical beauty. So if Isaiah says he wasn't' attractive, and yet he still was able to influence so many people, do you think you really need to hide your unique and weird traits?

Then there was another great influencer: Peter. He was a bare-knuckle dragger fisherman. Yeah, he was awkward and weird. He probably smelled like fish. But one thing is for darn sure: he didn't care. I personally think that's what made Jesus pick him to be one of His three closest guys. Peter didn't care that people were trying to shame him into keeping his mouth shut after Jesus rose from the dead, so he went for it!

> *Some, however, made fun of them and said, "They have had too much wine." Then Peter stood up with the Eleven, raised his voice and addressed the crowd: "Fellow Jews and all of you who live in Jerusalem, let me explain this to you; listen carefully to what I say. These people are not drunk, as you suppose. It's only nine in the morning! No, this is what was spoken by the prophet Joel: "'In the last days, God says, I will pour out my Spirit on all people. Your sons and daughters will prophesy, your young men will see visions, your old men will dream dreams. (Acts 2:13–17)*

People were shaming the disciples about speaking in tongues and he didn't hesitate. He made no excuses but bypassed all the nonsense, waste-of time-words justifying the awkwardness of the situation and went right for truth.

HEY, MOSES HAD A LISP, JESUS WASN'T CONSIDERED ATTRACTIVE ACCORDING TO ISAIAH, PETER WAS A HAIRY CHESTED FISHERMAN, AND YOU...WELL, I SHOULDN'T SAY WHAT YOU ARE.

To close this chapter, if you're going to influence others, it's a lie that your weirdness will get in the way. There are three reasons someone will listen to you. You have a story. You have knowledge. You have a heart. So, rip open your soul and spirit and set your weirdness free!

Activation

Volunteer to get roasted as the head of your department. Throw a fundraiser party for a good cause and donate some of the money to the person who impersonates you the best—something along those lines. You could also ask your family members for feedback, what are your strengths and weaknesses, and weird aspects that no one mentions out loud.

This will give you incredible self-insight of how others think of you. Then harness that aspect like a pack of sled dogs driving through the snow. Surf it like a wave. Load it into your weapon to send a constant barrage of bullets at the enemy of your self-confidence and you be you!

CHAPTER 9

Team Mentality, Not Us Versus Them

Once we build our awareness and skills in leadership, we can use our influence to inspire teams at work. Have you ever seen a job posting for team-minded candidates? Almost everyone job posting says that. Yet I would suggest that being team minded does not come from the team members; it comes from the team leader.

I have seen the politics and drama of the workplace. When I worked for a security team guarding a very rich man, needless to say, politics and drama were on display every day. Everyone was shooting arrows at the target of 'climbing the corporate ladder.' So, I get it.

In most organizations, CEOs and corporate leaders who want to motivate their staff do so by designing employee compensation plans, advancement requirements, and bonuses. The desire is increasing the ROI by getting more out of each employee. With motivation comes productivity, and with productivity comes a competitive edge necessary to ensure a strong presence in the marketplace.

The instilled rewards program has a dark side though. For many people, as they climb the corporate ladder, they believe they can achieve greater success by pulling others down from their earned place on the ladder. They believe this frees up space on the rung they have their eyes set upon. Little do they know that pulling another person down reveals them to be unworthy of promotion or leadership positions. This kind of mentality actually disqualifies us without our knowing. If we truly want to be a leader, we should embody the sincere desire for our coworkers to succeed. IF THEY FEEL THAT FROM YOU, THEY WILL NATURALLY GRAVITATE TOWARD LETTING YOU LEAD THEM.

Military Side

In SEAL training, we go through an evolution called Hell Week. This notoriously is revered as the toughest of all challenges the military can give someone. It consists of five days and five nights of continuous exercise. Hell week simulates a war-like environment and is notably the hardest part of the six-month-long Basic Underwater

Demolition (BUDs) school. The second night of Hell Week leads into Third Dawn which is a well-known milestone students strive to reach.

Everyone who is going to quit has probably done so before Third Dawn. Everybody remaining in the class, statistically, will forge the rest of training and get the honor to wear that bird on their chest. At this point, you can assume that the men standing next to you will go on to complete BUD/S and become Navy SEALs, at least by a large high ninety's percentage.

I remember going out to the beach the second night, we had been going forty-eight hours without sleep or rest. About 20 logs were lined up perpendicular to the ocean, waiting for us. One for each of the 20 boat crews of students left in my class. In each boat crew were seven students. The instructor staff lined us up next to the logs and said an interesting thing: "Do not drop the log on your head."

I thought to myself, "What an interesting thing to say. Who would drop a log on their own head? But okay, I'll try not to." It was a bit like someone telling you not to tie your shoes together. We later learned why.

They instructed every boat crew team to pick up the log and put it above their heads at full extension. We did, and immediately the chaos of instructors yelling silenced. This was the first time in two days we weren't being yelled at. The truck sirens were quieted, the megaphones weren't yelling at someone. Silence. I was then able to hear the sound of the ocean waves again about fifty feet away. In that moment of intense training, I can remember how beautiful the sound of nature was.

But no order came to put the log down. One minute went by… Two minutes went by… The sound of the Pacific Ocean waves was forgotten as our breathing grew harder… Three minutes went by. The instructor staff said nothing, and those logs were getting heavy.

Then the whimpering started. Teeth ground together as students felt fatigue building in their shoulders. There were some groans and murmurs; some coming from my mouth too. Then I heard something I haven't forgotten as if it is seared into my mind— the voices of grown men calling for their moms. No kidding, this was the breaking point. This was the second night preceding the Third Dawn and a last push to become a SEAL. This would get the quitters out and discover who the true warriors were. Four minutes went by and still no command to put the logs down.

At this point, arms were bending, and logs were starting to sag. The instructor staff came back into play and would make their way to boat crews who had sinking logs. Generally the lower end of a log and ask the students why the log was sinking right above their heads.

As the log above my head began to drop, I tried to push it back up, but it kept sinking. A green face appeared in front of my right eyeball. I could feel his breath. I had no idea who this instructor was as my focus was on getting the log back up. He asked me, "Is it you or is it the person in front of you letting the log drop?" There really is no right answer to that question. But there was one wrong one! That would have been to blame the person in front of or behind me. IN TRAINING, YOU NEVER BLAME THE GUY BESIDE YOU. I responded with a lie, "Me instructor", I shouted. I honestly thought it was the guy in front of me because I had been carrying his weight a little the last few days.

One thing you are taught in SEAL training is that you never blame your buddy or give him up…ever. Doing so marks you with a huge target on your back for being a traitor to the instructors and their job is to weed you out of the program. And they will get you to quit. Their tactics to do this are never fun to watch.

This instructor was checking to see if I had learned this yet. It is a question you can only find the answer to at the point of adversity and extreme discomfort. He ordered me to put the log back up or he was going to pull me out of training, never to return. The fear of failure filled my body, and to my surprise, I pushed the log back to the sky. My arms straightened. I was relieved, enlightened and happy.

IT WAS THEN, IN THAT MOMENT OF PAIN, WEAK-NESS AND QUESTIONING MYSELF THAT HE HAD JUST INTRODUCED ME TO MYSELF.

They were using this evolution to bring teamwork to the sur-face and see who had the team mentality and who would blame those around them. Slowly the minutes passed. Six minutes, then seven.

Serious pain was setting into our muscles and joints. Groaning and grunting grew louder. Every breath in and out of our mouths was being pushed out and sucked back in, in an effort to take our minds off of how bad our legs and arms hurt.

Then the instructors swooped in and introduced the next component to becoming an elite warrior. They demanded silence. "Suffer in silence!" the instructor staff insisted. Not a sound was allowed. COMPLETE PAIN WAS PAIRED WITH COMPLETE SILENCE. IT HAS MUCH THE SAME SOUND AS A PEACE-FUL WALK THROUGH THE FOREST ON A STILL NIGHT. SILENCE DOESN'T ALWAYS TELL A STORY; IT HIDES IT.

As the boat crew teams started to bobble their logs up and down, the instructors reminded us that it pays to be a winner and the winning boat crew team would be awarded with sitting out whatever came next.

As ten minutes went by, logs started dropping to the ground. It suddenly made sense why the instructors had said not to drop the log on our heads. We all made sure to let it down slow, keeping our skulls from getting crushed.

While all the losing teams were waiting for the last few boat crews to find out who won, we were instructed to bury our logs in the sand using our boat paddles as shovels. When we were done burying them, we could then dig them back up and take them into the ocean to clean them off in the surf zone. Once we got them all clean, we could then bring them back and bury them again.

Once the winning team stood alone, having completed what seemed like about fifteen minutes, the training staff revealed what came next. We were instructed to look south down the beach where we could see a point eight miles away. The challenge was for us to race down to that point, carrying our logs every step of the way. The crew who had won the last challenge did not have to participate for the first mile. They got to put their log in the back of the truck and ride down ahead of everyone else. The first team to reach the point was a new winner and would not have to do what came next. The second boat crew team to arrive would be the first loser.

As we ran down the beach, we employed different forms of carrying the log. As a team, we chose to carry the log on our shoulders and kept switching shoulders as we went, but that rubbed our shoulders raw. Some of us chose to carry the log in front of us, but that only made our biceps and backs burn. Some teams chose to do quick sprints and rest while others chose to set into a good steady march.

As promised, the first boat crew team down there got to put their log in the truck and sit down for a break. Everyone else who lost were to stand there and hold their log until everyone arrived. Yes, it does pay to be a winner.

At about midnight down on the edge of the ocean, we fought the fatigue and ate our midrats (midnight rations) and waited for the instructors to tell us what was next. Too soon, they lined us up facing north and said we were to carry the logs back. The first team back would win and would not have to do what comes next. Always, it pays to be a winner.

As the sun was coming up, we all returned with our logs and were met by the winners of the first race. That was Third Dawn and we were pretty sure the men still standing there would also go on to complete Hell Week, BUDs and become a SEAL. IT WAS A GUT-WRENCHING SELF-TRIAL OF FINDING OUT WHO

YOU REALLY ARE DOWN DEEP INSIDE AND WHETHER

YOU ARE A TEAM PLAYER OR NOT.

The amount of work we did that night would never have been completed without working together as a team. Any infighting would have made this task worse and ultimately our team...unwinnable, to say the least.

As a good leader, your job is to put a team together who works effectively and efficiently together all while erasing the infighting. How do you inject a team mentality into your people? The goal here is to make a team that can operate together without micromanagement from you. As a leader, you should be such an awesome team player that you're able to help others do the same. As we say in the teams, "You can't ask someone to do something you haven't done yourself." This should be taken personally by everybody leading a team. So the answer to the question above, don't look to change the team, look to change yourself.

If the military's best is trained to operate in teams, do you think you are better off doing things by yourself or with a team? This is a military strategy that directly relates to our marketplace. A highly functioning team will do much more productive work than will a team with hidden complaints, dramas, and competitions.

"But, Charles," you may say, "in the marketplace, I need to stand out among my team members to get promoted!"

Yes, but if you look at it with a hidden agenda of stepping on them instead of relying on your own professionalism and experience, success won't last. You'll only be planting a hidden time bomb of animosity in your team, ready to blow up and destroy what you guys did together. You may be followed around by gossip following the team's separation. The secret here for you is that if you work well with others and support them, they will elevate you as a leader or manager organically. They will give you a peer promotion sometime, somewhere in the future. That is way better than grabbing each opportunity available to you to brownnose or tattletale like a child for promotion. You will grow your reputation as well as your team's effectiveness. THAT TIME BOMB OF ANIMOSITY IN YOUR PEERS WILL TURN INTO PEER PROMOTION.

Biblical Perspective

The Bible has much to say about putting the team before yourself, but most of it is shown and not told. For example, Jesus himself who is the head of the team left his position in heaven to put himself below every one of his team members on earth. Because honestly, if he never humbled himself to be slain and sacrificed, his team wouldn't be the same. Saved, sanctified, and empowered. No, he didn't have to do it. Yes, he did.

He also said in Matthew 12:25, "Every kingdom divided against itself will be ruined, and every city or household divided against itself will not stand."

This, too, is true because how can something grow evenly if tended unequally? How can someone lead a team when each of the team's members has an agenda to outrank all the others on the team?

However, there is room for testing. I love the untold team-work displayed when Paul was a team player and he opposed Cephas (Peter) to his face.

When Cephas came to Antioch, I opposed him to his face, because he stood condemned.
(Galatians 2:11)

Peter and Paul had a disagreement. It doesn't really matter what it was about honestly, but Paul, whose heart was on fire to see the team advance correctly, called out Peter. This is okay because it isn't about rank or status a person has on the team. It's about the mission. Both of these men talked out their differences to further the mission, and both were completely satisfied with their position. This argument wasn't infighting; it was teamwork, a focus on their cause.

Yet there were the "sons of thunder" who did care about position.

> *Then the mother of Zebedee's sons came to Jesus with her sons and, kneeling down, asked a favor of him. "What is it you want?" he asked. She said, "Grant that one of these two sons of mine may sit at your right and the other at your left in your kingdom." "You don't know what you are asking," Jesus said to them. "Can you drink the cup I am going to drink?" "We can," they answered. Jesus said to them, "You will indeed drink from my cup, but to sit at my right or left is not for me to grant. These places belong to those for whom they have been prepared by my Father." When the ten heard about this, they were indignant with the two brothers. Jesus called them together and said, "You know that the rulers of the Gentiles lord it over them, and their high officials exercise authority over them. Not so with you. Instead, whoever wants to become great among you must be your servant, and whoever wants to be first must be your slave—just as the Son of Man*

did not come to be served, but to serve, and to give his life

as a ransom for many."

(Matthew 20:20–28)

Did you catch the mic drop moment? "You don't know what you're asking." "To sit at my right or left side and drink of my cup," Jesus was talking about future martyrdom. But the lesson of teamwork is the same. In order to elevate the team, your team must be above you. You can take it to the bank.

Activation

Today I want you to get better at self-evaluation. Check this out. We are going to focus on gossip. If you hear someone gossiping, don't join in as that is a sign that you are internally not a good team player or team leader. That's right. It's one of the most successful enemies of growing a good team. If a person is gossiping to you and there's absolutely no escaping, I want you to tee up your golf shot like this. It's one of my favorite ways out of such situations. Simply say,

"That sounds like me. At times I am just like that very thing
and I'm trying to personally work on it."

A SIMPLE LITMUS TEST TO KNOW IF YOU'RE GOSSIPING OR NOT IS THIS: IF IT FEELS GOOD DON'T SAY IT. That's right. If what you say makes you feel justified while someone else isn't and that makes you feel elevated above others, don't let it slip.

Consider today a detox from gossip and judgment. Get ready for an explosive growth of your reputation because after all, we are leading others in a "good direction."

CHAPTER 10

Know Why People Follow You

Good leaders know their teams and they know why people follow. And it may be different from person to person. What do your followers get by following you? Money? A strong purpose? Wisdom? Popularity? A family relationship? Safety?

Pause and Answer.

Whatever it may be, without knowing why people follow, can make it difficult to motivate them. Not knowing your leverage makes it even harder to grow your company or group. You may also have a ticking time bomb waiting for you that could rob you of all your hard work. Let me explain.

Let's consider a fitness coach as an example of this principle. People pay you money to work out with your instruction. Why do they follow you? To get fitness results? Yes, but having been in the fitness industry I would say mostly no. The way I see it, people want to feel good about themselves and leave with a smile. I promise you, in most cases, results in body composition fall second to how you lift their spirits during a workout session. People's fitness goals change but they always want to laugh, smile, and vent a little about life. So, the reason a fitness coach has a following is not what it appears to be at first glance.

This is how 'not knowing why people follow you' can cause a problem. Let's say a coach comes to work one day without sleep, tired, and lacking the motivation to put on a smile. The coach will have trouble giving their clients energy; they're going to deprive them of energy. The coach might as well give them a crying baby to hold for an hour as it will yield a similar outcome. In this case, a fitness coach should know that people follow them for more than fitness results and cause retention problems if they don't learn.

Marketplace

Let's consider a few more examples about why people follow others. Specifically Internships.

A newly graduated college student will work an internship with no pay for a while. They do this for a few reasons:

1. It promises a future job.

2.   It builds a résumé.

3.   Gets them experience.

4.   They haven't yet established their self-worth.

That's four reasons kids will work for no money. All of those could be leveraged by a company, or you, in various ways to leverage productivity and further your cause of leading people in a good direction.

This is like many volunteer scenarios. People volunteer for good causes all the time. Political causes and nonprofit causes like cancer fundraising are two of many that people will work for without pay. Why do people volunteer?

1.   Bragging rights and conversation starters.

2.   A belief in the cause.

3.   Meet people with similar desires.

4.   Change the world.

5.   Résumé building.

The list goes on. I will say it again because I see it all the time. If you're the head of a group of volunteers who really believe in the cause, be very careful stewarding their trust! There may be circumstances that you don't think are advantageous for you or the organization, but I say those little events and details are. Maybe more important than the big ones. You have to think long term, not short-term, to leverage your situation and see the value in always leading your people the right ways and doing the right thing.

Military Side

During my time in Naval Special Warfare, there was a military bond. Not many people know this, but the job of Navy SEAL is voluntary. During training and throughout my career, I could quit at any time. You can lay down your trident and sail the high seas in the Navy anytime you wish.

Once, before a dangerous mission, a team member in our community walked away from his duties and the brothers on his team. I bring this fact to your attention because it's different from the rest of DOD (Department of Defense) members. In the rest of the military, if you were to desert your duties, you would be court-martialed (arrested, charged and tried) and serve sometime in the brig (military jail). I'm not sure which I would rather have: the court-martial or having to look into my brothers' eyes as they load up on the choppers for a dangerous mission without me knowing I might have made a difference to their success.

For this example, let's put the Teams to the side and focus on the units of the military who don't have a voluntary option and must follow orders. The reason people serve in most military units and obey orders here is two-fold. First, you would pay dearly for neglecting an order. Second, you get promoted by following orders. A military leader can use fear in their leading as well as promotion incentives. Even though it works and works well in the military, I wouldn't use dangling the "fear carrot" in the marketplace. It is harmful to people and really just shows that you're a simple-minded leader if you use it. A bit of a "play how I want or I'm taking my ball and going home" attitude.

What does this look like? Any kind of demeaning, ignoring, "'cuz I said so" attitude or yelling is simple-minded fear-based leadership. The only requirement for leading someone in the military is more bars on your shoulder than theirs. It doesn't require much wisdom to direct people around you.

For some, when they get out of the military, find themselves at a loss. You see, most veterans learned fear-based leadership. Hopefully, as a leader, you can say that people follow you because you inspire them in a good way, not because they are afraid of consequences. Military veterans have been wired in the first way and probably don't know they have been taught and wired differently than the civilian world. As a leader, hopefully, you bring smiles to your people and they don't just show up for work for a paycheck because they see no other immediate option.

Biblical Perspective

> *Be sure you know the condition of your flocks, give careful attention to your herds; for riches do not endure forever, and a crown is not secure for all generations. (Proverbs 27:23–24)*

King Saul was a man who fell prey to this principle and his crown was lost after just one generation. During his life, he had no idea why David followed him.

> *Now Saul's daughter Michal was in love with David, and when they told Saul about it, he was pleased. "I will give her to him," he thought, "so that she may be a snare to him and so that the hand of the Philistines may be against him." So Saul said to David, "Now you have a second opportunity to become my son-in-law." Then Saul ordered his attendants: "Speak to David privately and say, 'Look, the king likes you, and his attendants all love you; now become his son-in law.'" They repeated*

these words to David. But David said, "Do you think

it is a small matter to become the king's son-in-law? I'm

only a poor man and little known." When Saul's servants

told him what David had said, Saul replied, "Say to

David, 'The king wants no other price for the bride than

a hundred Philistine foreskins, to take revenge on his ene-

mies.'" Saul's plan was to have David fall by the hands

of the Philistines. When the attendants told David these

things, he was pleased to become the king's son-in-law. So

before the allotted time elapsed, David took his men with

him and went out and killed two hundred Philistines and

brought back their foreskins. They counted out the full

number to the king so that David might become the king's

son-in-law. Then Saul gave him his daughter Michal in

marriage. (1 Samuel 18:20–27)

You see, when David was a young boy, King Saul summoned him to play a harp and ease his mood. Saul thought it was because of payment that David was there but he is mistaken; it was because Samuel had anointed him to take the throne one day. When David stepped forward to kill Goliath, King Saul thought it was because he had promised the man who slew the giant would be tax-free in the land, but no. It was because the Lord was leading him to save the Country-of-the-One-True-God. And here, Saul still had no idea that David was there because of his calling and not for money. The proof is when David said, "I'm only a poor man." Meaning, I don't have any money to purchase his daughter for marriage. Indeed, he was poor, but indeed he wasn't there for money. A deadly miscalculation for King Saul's legacy. Although he used his daughter as a trap (he was sick in the head), the Lord turned it around for David's good.

Now on the flip side, there are some stories that pop out to me as interesting. In a world that is built on recognition and social media followers, most people don't even stop to consider that in some cases it's better to not have a following at all. There were times that Jesus wanted to prevent people from following him. Why? They were coming after him for the wrong reasons.

> *When Jesus saw the crowd around him, he gave orders to cross to the other side of the lake. Then a teacher of the law came to him and said, "Teacher, I will follow you wherever you go." Jesus replied, "Foxes have dens and birds have nests, but the Son of Man has no place to lay his head." Another disciple said to him, "Lord, first let me go and bury my father." But Jesus told him, "Follow*

me, and let the dead bury their own dead." Then he got

into the boat and his disciples followed him. (Matthew

8:18–23)

Let me ask you. Do you have the wisdom and foresight to turn one of your followers around and say, "Go, it's not time"?

Something to consider, something to ponder in this ever so fast-moving culture. I suggest to stop and access someone else's reasons for following a great leader like you and get your mind off our yourself, your money, your purpose and your belongings.

And you, my leader friends, do you know why people follow you? Don't try to change their reasons. Don't try to draw them closer for the wrong reasons. And don't try to push them away for the wrong reasons either. With each who follows, you must use your discernment and look at the bigger picture.

Activation

What's the bond of your followers? Why do people follow you? Let's go through these three steps.

1. Circle all that apply.
    a. Money
    b. Family ties
    c. Security
    d. You inspire them.
    e. They are brownnosing you to climb the corporate ladder.
    f. You're a résumé builder.
    g. They care about your cause.
    h. They want to marry you.
    i. They are stealing money from your accounts.
    j. They are a spy.
    k. Job experience.
    l. Sense of value.
    m. _____

2. Now that you've identified these, learn how to leverage this information in a way that leads people in a good direction. Also, try to remove the negative leadership qualities in your organization that are based on fear. People should choose to follow without those motivating factors present.

3. Don't forget these reasons and never take your followers for granted after today.

CHAPTER 11

Steer the Ship When Necessary—Otherwise, Get Out of the Way

When I owned my CrossFit gym in Washington, we had a prominent local public figure take on the challenge of our fitness routine. He was a pastor at one of the largest congregations in the area. I knew if he were to stick with the program, thousands of people would notice and then possibly consider our program as well. When he finished his five mandatory fundamental classes, his next class happened to be with our largest, most intense coach.

My friend and coach is six-feet-four-inches-tall, has a long beard, is an ex-marine, and possesses the type A attitude to match. As our newest member, the pastor nervously showed up. The mammoth coach shouted at the pastor, "Sir, do you like being yelled at?"

I thought for sure we had lost the pastor. The pastor brushed it off and responded, "Well, I don't know if I do or not. We'll have to find out."

When they glanced over at me, I said, "Sometimes you have to steer the ship, and this isn't one of those times" Then I shook my head at my type A mammoth of a friend and got out of his way to lead class.

You see, the reason my behemoth friend felt comfortable enough to use those words and tone with the pastor while teaching the class was because I had given him the freedom to coach in the manner he saw fit. (Which could easily change from class to class depending on the variables important to the coach himself.) I EVEN GLORIFIED AND CELEBRATED MY COACHES FOR THEIR STYLES. One of the best ways to get the best performance or effort out of someone is to give them the freedom to do what is best in their minds in the way that best suits them. It's a principle of freedom. Freedom works. You see, my goal was to keep the atmosphere fun and friendly, and to do that you have to pick your battles. Treat minor things with minor engagement and major things with a friendly direct conversation on the side.

Funny enough, the local pastor did stick out the program and became a regularly attending member for years.

Military Side

While serving in the Teams, we would be tasked with an objective and build a mission around the task we were given. As a top-tier asset, we were given a good measure of trust to complete the mission. With that trust we also had the ability and creativity to complete what we were tasked to, however we wanted or needed to. I want you to notice that the freedom we were allowed to conduct the mission is separate from the rest of the military. We weren't tied to the same formalities that exist in the rest of the military, and I would say that led to our success on the mission field. One of our sayings in the teams was "shiny boots don't make you good at your job." It was almost as if the Department of Defense knew that to get us to perform our best, they had to release us to do it with our own creativity. In a way, they steered the ship when necessary and got out of the way for the rest. The overall mission was accomplished, but we were trusted to figure out the details of how.

I remember gearing up for a certain mission we were conducting. None of our intelligence collection methods were dictated to us, except those from the Geneva convention, overarching rules of engagement and proper military practices. We were given information collecting technology, insertion and extraction platforms as well as large amounts of training to be successful. We were not told how to arrange the mission at all, in any way. We used the freedom to "go and do" what we needed to do using our tools and knowledge.

Marketplace

There are decentralized and centralized business plans. If you're reading this and already have a bit of marketplace experience, you most likely don't need an explanation of what the difference is between those two entities' modalities.

A centralized business plan is one that outlines everything someone will do and how they will do it. A mountain of bureaucracy is enlisted to keep every process and employee movement organized and run just right. An example of this would be a fast-food chain sandwich shop. Their business plan would likely outline exactly how to make each sandwich, what uniform to wear, and what price to charge.

On the other end of the spectrum, a decentralized business is one that doesn't control any of the methods people use to do business; they just require a fee for being affiliated. An example of this would be a sporting goods store that lets store managers fill their stores with items that are relevant to that particular region. Most decisions are still made at the headquarters, but managers are given more freedom to be more competitive.

The difference is that a centralized company is great until demand surges. There is no way for it to expand rapidly. It must become decentralized to expand to keep up with demand.

In the same way, you must give people the freedom to be creative to expand your influence. Your leadership style should be more of a decentralized style than a centralized style. Controlling everything around you will do the opposite of what you actually desire and create a small time-bomb.

Let's personalize this principle so you can apply it to your life and professional growth. Are you spending your time controlling situations that don't need to be controlled? Why? I dare you to answer honestly.

MICROMANAGING IS SOMETHING MANAGERS DO, NOT LEADERS. Employ freedom and steer the ship when necessary; otherwise, get out of the way. You'll be glad you did and you'll also be able to relax more.

Biblical Perspective

Having enough faith to give people freedom in the workplace is a huge overarching principle in the Bible yet is difficult to find directly expressed in the scriptures unless you accompany your reading with prayer and meditation.

The Bible says whatever you do will prosper (Psalms 1). It is when we don't have faith in this promise of God's that we try to overcontrol our situations and business. As a leader, if you'd like to witness to people about your faith but are overcontrolling people in the workplace, it shows others that you really don't believe in a God that is leading the course of your cause and business. Let me show this to you with a question.

Why did a good God put a way out for Adam and Eve in the garden of Eden? If, in fact, everything was "good" and contained a harmonious everlasting population, then why would he allow this? Everything was good. Everything was in harmony. Yet a tree was given to Adam and Eve as a way out.

The woman said to the serpent, "We may
eat fruit from the trees in the garden, but God
did say, 'You must not eat fruit from the tree that

is in the middle of the garden, and you must not

touch it, or you will die.'" (Genesis 3:2)

The answer is that God started creation with an especially important mechanism in place: freedom. He gave humans the choice to follow him or to walk away from him. He will never take your freedom to choose away from you.

This is an important ingredient for God to use because without freedom, it is not true love. If people are forced to follow God, it is not a true following.

I would suggest that if the Creator God uses freedom in his leadership practices, we might want to as well by constructing social-engineered ways for people to act under our authority.

This is one of the beginning principles in the Bible and one of the last principles of the Bible. I'd imagine it exists all throughout as well.

Let the one who does wrong continue to do wrong;
let the vile person continue to be vile; let the one who does
right continue to do right; and let the holy person continue
to be holy.

(Revelation 22:10–11)

Now go forth, my great leader friend, and stop choking the heads off your chickens. Let them run and have fun. They will love you for it.

Activation

Try this: next time someone comes and asks you a question, put it back on them. Ask, "How do you think it should be done?" You will watch them grow right before your eyes.

Also, try to steer clear of any micro decision-making for others. Allow them to bring their own flavor to your cause. Hopefully, you notice them come alive in the process.

CHAPTER 12

Complaining Versus Offering Solutions

When you read the news, sometimes it can feel like the only things reported are terrible, depressing events. Why do you think the media concentrates on the bad things in life rather than the good?

It isn't that negative events are the only things that happen. Positive things occur as well. So perhaps journalists are drawn to reporting bad news because sudden disaster is more compelling than slow improvements. Or it could be that newsgatherers believe that cynical reports of unfortunate events make for simpler stories and less time researching.

Consider for a moment a thought I will justify in the rest of this chapter. Our negative tendencies are a large part of what is wrong with America today. In business, in sports, in all of life, and the news we digest—there is a lot of handwringing, hopelessness, and blaming others to the point of whining and—just complaining. It's the focus and overfocusing on these things that bring us down in more ways than one. Many more ways, but this is the tip of the iceberg.

COMPLAINING IS WHAT IMMATURE CHILDREN DO. IT BRINGS ALL KINDS OF EMOTIONS AND ATTITUDES INTO THE SPOTLIGHT. OFFERING SOLUTIONS FOR PROBLEMS IN A PROFESSIONAL MANNER IS WHAT LEADERS DO.

So why would there be many more news articles that simulate complaining rather than offer suggestions? Here lies another principle and you need to decide which side of the fence you would like to position yourself on as a leader. The gauge of this principle is "If it's easier, it's most likely not the right choice."

Is it easier to build a house to code or build a house and cut some corners? Is it easier to suck it up and take blame when you're wrong or pass the blame on to someone else? Is it easier to finish a project or to start a project? Is it easier to complain or is it easier to put your neck on the line and publicly submit a solution? In the same way, it's easier for a journalist to report on negative news rather than report on solutions for a problem. That, plus it probably gets more clicks, likes, and follows. If it bleeds, it reads.

POINT IS, IF WE ARE DOING THE EASY THING WE ARE PROBABLY NOT LEADING.

Marketplace

In 2014 while I owned my CrossFit gym, I suddenly had a land-lord issue and had to move my gym and all the equipment from one side of the parking lot to the other. This triggered the need to submit a building permit. Each new building permit submitted to the city also required a new sidewalk to be constructed. Also, placement of a water main, electrical, and sewer lines underneath the sidewalk, which would have cost hundreds of thousands of dollars. A business like mine would have been put under, but it was the law.

For six months, I fought with the city code enforcement officer without any progress. Disputing with the building code enforcement officer is like arguing with a police officer to get out of the traffic ticket. It doesn't work. I went to the city council and attempted to change the laws to prevent the current laws from shutting me down. They weren't business-friendly laws, and I was sure the city wanted to know ways of attracting more businesses.

I became a subject matter expert regarding the building codes so I could suggest a solution, not complain. I blew the trumpet and seventy of our members showed up to a Monday night council meeting with a suggestion, not a complaint. Might I add that it was quite a sight? There were seventy of us which was more than the thirty or so chairs they had set up for the public to sit in.

A complaint would not have helped. It's like this. Complaining to city officials about being put out of business doesn't tell them what they can do to fix a bad law; suggesting a change does and also gets you what you need in a more expeditious and appreciated manner.

On three pages of paper, I wrote the law as it stood, the problems it creates for small businesses, and how that affects the city by diminishing tax revenue. Finally, I wrote out measures that could be immediately taken to change how the needs of businesses could be met. I printed enough copies for each council member and my five-year-old son handed them out. That's what you call pure but unintentional manipulation. You should have seen their faces smiling at him as if it were their own grandson.

Then fifteen of our members used the public speaking time to express their opinions. Each had three minutes to explain why the council should pass the changes to the building code. I encouraged the younger athletes we had at our gym to practice public speaking in front of the city council. Some were twelveor thirteen-year-old girls, and they won the hearts of the seated local officials.

You could see each council member being transformed into a proud civil servant promoting the young to get involved in local legislation. They were filled with glee and even gave a few head nods to the teenagers who were a bit nervous. The city passed the suggestion 7–0 saving my business and almost three hundred thousand dollars.

After the meeting, the council members approached me and said that usually when people come for their three minutes of public speaking time to address the council, they yell at us and tell us how dumb we are. They said our group was all smiling and happy and that's exactly what they wanted in their city.

That's the power of suggestion versus complaining. Please recognize suggestion as an influencer and leader! If and when you become a leader, you'll have to stop childish ways of outlining things that are wrong, and in its place, suggest change.

Biblical Perspective

If there is any complaining coming out of your mouth, it only means that you have previously somehow been disconnected from Jesus's ways. Complaining to others is like telling God he can't handle the things in your life or he isn't real. Paul tells us a little secret about this one.

> *I know what it is to be in need, and I know what it is to have plenty. I have learned the secret of being content in any and every situation, whether well fed or hungry, whether living in plenty or in want. I can do all this through him who gives me strength. (Philippians 4:12–13)*

If we are complaining, we are not "in him" at that moment. Good thing there is grace. As Christians, we have to know that the Holy Spirit takes us through different seasons to add things to our lives. Unaware of that fact, we can spiral into trying to take things back into our own hands in stressful times.

When I exited the Navy, the Holy Spirit knew I had too much pride in my life. God is good at putting us right in situations that force us to deal with our sins. We may be in a position in life that we'd rather not be in, but we also need to recognize the opportunity of sanctification at hand, and that God calls us to "be Holy as he is Holy."

It was 2009 when I began working in private security. All new hires had to start on the night shift. This was humbling to go from being a Navy SEAL to working nights under some of these guys, most of whom had no real experience. I worked for a guy who was an ex-marine who, for whatever reason, didn't like Navy SEALs. He was enthralled that he was in charge of one, in charge of me. He used every possible opportunity to publicly defame me in front of the team for anything he could. At the time, I didn't like it, but looking back, I can see God's hand all over it.

One day when I was carrying out my duties, a coworker came to me and asked if I had just seen the latest team e-mail from this guy. I said no and checked my phone to read it. It let everyone know that I had left some of the blinds open the day before and how we should pay more attention to details and a few other "descriptive" words. He obviously did not need to email everyone my mistake. But as a leader, with about 100 percent of his leadership knowledge from the military, he was defining himself.

I had been strategically placed in this spot at this time to work on my humility. My reply was to thank God for this moment. I didn't grumble to my coworker. I didn't slander my boss behind his back, but instead I blessed him. Also, in that moment, something came up out of my spirit and I saw that it was my marine manager who was in the pain.

After I read the email, my coworker was waiting for a response. You know, the "off the record just between me and you" response. I said, "It looks like God was wanting to work on my humility." He expected me to say something different, something in anger. Yet God had me in this season to deal with my pride.

He was stunned, and as a self-proclaimed atheist, he said something interesting: "You Christians never have lows. Even when bad things happen to you, it's still good." MIGHT IT BE THAT PART OF EVANGELISM IS WITHHOLDING COMPLAINTS?

The Bible does not hide this principle behind any need for prayer and fasting for understanding. It says it outright. You're not given a choice to decide to be a complainer or someone who makes suggestions; you're given a two-by-four to the head. A learn by drinking from a firehose school of hard knocks kind of learning.

> *And Moses said, "When the Lord gives you in the evening meat to eat and in the morning bread to the full, because the Lord has heard your grumbling that you grumble against him—what are we? Your grumbling is not against us but against the Lord." (Exodus 16:8)*

Now the people complained about their hardships in the hearing of the LORD, and when he heard them his anger was aroused. Then fire from the LORD burned among them and consumed some of the outskirts of the camp. When the people cried out to Moses, he prayed to the LORD and the fire died down. So that place was called Taberah, because fire from the LORD had burned among them. The rabble with them began to crave other food, and again the Israelites started wailing and said, "If only we had meat to eat!" (Numbers 11:1–4)

Do not be conformed to this world, but be transformed by the renewal of your mind, that by testing you may discern what is the will of God, what is good and acceptable and perfect. (Romans 12:2)

And we know that for those who love God all things work together for good, for those who are called according to his purpose. (Romans 8:28)

Nor grumble, as some of them did and were destroyed by the Destroyer. (1 Corinthians 10:10, Paul is referring to the Israelites in Numbers 11)

Do all things without grumbling or questioning, that you may be blameless and innocent, children of God without blemish in the midst of a crooked and twisted generation, among whom you shine as lights in the world, holding fast to the word of life, so that in the day of Christ I may be proud that I did not run in vain or labor in vain. (Philippians 2:14–16)

Give thanks in all circumstances; for this is the will of God in Christ Jesus for you. (1 Thessalonians 5:18)

Let no corrupting talk come out of your mouths, but only such as is good for building up.
(Ephesians 4:29)

Show hospitality to one another without grumbling.
(1 Peter 4:9)

Do not grumble against one another, brothers, so that you may not be judged; behold, the Judge is standing at the door. (James 5:9)

Activation

If you are a complainer, how could you know? Here's how we'll find out.

Go back through your own social media threads and score yourself. Count how many times you complained, ranted, or pointed something negative out. In the other column, count how many suggestions or positive remarks you made. Let the numbers speak for themselves. Numbers don't lie.

Positive Suggestions	Negative Complaints or Idle Comments

CHAPTER 13

That Sounds Like Me

These days it's all about judging and judging people harshly. Just sit back and consider it. People sit on the panel of American Idol and judge each contender. Teachers judge students' test scores and give them a grade. On Yelp or Google, if we didn't like the service, we write a bad review. Our days are filled with judging information pertaining to other people.

As the leader of a group of people, it should be important to recognize strengths and weaknesses. Please consider that noticing strengths and weaknesses in people is very different than judging. Judging is tied to emotions, mostly negative emotions. And when that judging becomes public between two or more people, that is called gossip or slander. A LEADER WHO WANTS TO BUILD

A GOOD REPUTATION MUST AVOID GOSSIPING AND, IN ITS PLACE, CREATE A LOYALTY TO THE ABSENT.

The definition of gossip is talking about someone behind their back in agreement with others. This is cancer in so many ways to the one speaking and should be avoided at all times. Many people think the harm is done to the one being gossiped about—wrong; the harm corrodes the one letting the words fly. By the way, do you know how to tell if you've hired a gossip or if someone is gossiping about you?

A GOOD WAY TO KNOW IF SOMEONE IS GOING TO TALK ABOUT YOU IS SHOWN WHEN THEY TALK ABOUT SOMEONE ELSE TO YOU.

It doesn't just show their disapproval in judging others; it shows them to have disregard for others regardless of who it is, you included.

The drama and existence of people chatting aside, if you have employees or volunteers working for you and they continually fail to meet goals or are underperforming their duties, this isn't necessarily a bad thing. It could be a good thing.

The absence of employee performance brings a new ability and tool you as a leader must be aware of. An opportunity often unnoticed.

AS A LEADER YOU'RE TRYING TO HELP YOUR PEO-PLE ACHIEVE A LEVEL OF SELF-ACTUALIZATION AND ACHIEVEMENT ABOVE WHAT THEY THOUGHT POSSI-BLE. As you elevate your ability as a leader, you'll learn how to facilitate other people's personal and professional growth.

How can you recognize those around you who might need help growing or reevaluating their position in your company? Check it out. There is a way to find them like a laser-guided missile. Gossipers point them out. They will say things about them like, "That person just can't put two and two together" or "That person is up the creek without a paddle." Maybe you've heard it like this: "That person just doesn't have the knack for the job." Really, what a leader (you) should be saying is: "That person is going to make their contribution one day, once they find their spot and skill."

PLACING SOMEONE IN THE POSITION THAT THEY LIKE OFTEN MAKES THEM ONE OF THE MOST PRODUC-TIVE EMPLOYEES YOU HAVE. Just because they're not good at one thing doesn't mean that you should slam them with it. It means you may have to move them around in your company to find a better fit. It's good because you're about to stumble upon a way to make your company more productive and even better, helping them find themselves in the process and building trust and loyalty at the same time.

Marketplace

Why do we think this does not applies only to adults? We see this principle in kids very early. We label our kids with learning disorders like ADD or ADHD. Sometimes we medicate them. We will label them with social disorders and agree that something isn't wired right in their brains. I would suggest that child might just need a different learning atmosphere. Did you know that a vast majority of CEOs were only C students in high school?

There once was a middle school girl who wasn't doing well at a private school as a student in the early 1900s in London. One day the principal called her parents for a meeting. As they sat and talked with the principal, he made the case of why the school was going to dismiss her and let someone else take her spot. They then called her in to give her the news. The principal had classical music playing in the background as they talked and he noticed her starting to sway in her chair to the music.

The principal, being a wise man, noticed her moving. He then focused on her and asked about her interests. He discovered that she wasn't "bad" at school; she just wasn't interested or passionate about it. So he suggested to her parents that she be enrolled in a music school. She then later became one of the leading play writers in London during the 1900s, ALL BECAUSE THE PRINCIPAL KNEW THIS LESSON OF RECOGNIZING AS A LEADER, WHAT PEOPLE ARE PASSIONATE FOR, and where they should invest their talents.

I hope you gain the same wisdom as this middle school principal had while reading this chapter.

Let's look at another marketplace example.

Case Study:

Jeremy Lin was one of the first Asian basketball players to play in the NBA. You may have heard of the term people made about him: "LINSANITY." He stands about a foot taller than both of his parents and naturally started to play the game of basketball and pursued a career. His early career brought about some humbling times.

He was traded back and forth between the third and fourth position on basketball teams and then down to the development league for years. He got traded mid-season to the Knicks of the 2011–12 season as a fourth-string point guard. On some rosters, his name wasn't even listed. His dreams came true when the unfortunate happened to the two-point guards ahead of him.

His coach D'Antoni turned to him in desperation after they lost eleven of thirteen games that season. What happened next was completely unexpected. The next day, Lin scored twenty-five points and led his team to a win against the Nets and the players described him as having a "rhyme and a reason" for what he was doing to the team.

The next game Lin scored twenty-eight points to beat the Utah Jazz. Later in the season, Lin scored thirty-eight points against the Lakers and Kobe Bryant at a time when Kobe had never even heard of him. Jeremy Lin became the very first NBA player to score at least seven points and have seven assists in each of his first five starts.

Why was Jeremy Lin's NBA debut so amazing? Why had all those other teams who employed him not recognized his ability?

Lin gives us the truth of the matter in a speech he gave to his local church. LIN SAID THAT THE KNICKS RAN THE TYPE OF OFFENSE THAT HE LIKED PLAYING THE BEST. A FAST-PACED OFFENSE THAT FIT HIS STYLE.

This should rock everyone who claims to be a leader to the core. The reason Jeremy Lin had been so looked over as a player was because coaches looked at him from a standpoint of "how can this person fit into our system" and not how he plays best. Again, this should rock you to your core as a leader. What frustrates me most about this is that Lin played under so many coaches, scouts, and leaders of their profession, and they still were unable to see this person for what he was able to do when playing ball his way, with a fast offense.

Let me ask you: what do you think people said about him behind closed doors? Let me tell you. Some said the NBA only brought him on so that Asians would buy his jersey. Some said he was too skinny. Were they right? Maybe, but they weren't looking at him with the eyes of a 'good leader'. They missed it and a great player went undiscovered for two and a half years right in front of them.

Seriously, he was with the Knicks for three days before he played with them against the New Jersey Nets and led them to a turnaround season. A fluke? I think not. This is simply what happens when someone does something they were designed to do.

As a leader, don't join in with the gossip around the water cooler. Ask people what position that person would crush it in.

Let's say you have someone on the factory line who's slow in production because he over socializes. They come into work talking. They talk while they work and they talk after work. As their coworkers may gossip about them being too chatty, maybe consider moving them over to your sales department.

YOU WANT TO BE A GOOD LEADER? DON'T JUDGE
PEOPLE; GET CURIOUS ABOUT WHERE THEY MIGHT FIT.

Military Side

The popularity of SEAL training has grown over the last few decades because people have always wondered what makes the best soldier in the world. Basic Underwater Demolition school was formed around making a soldier capable of conducting warfare underwater, on top of the water, in the air, and on land.

Now the open ocean is a formidable force and the ultimate equalizer to all men, both strong and proud. Even if you're only enjoying it recreationally, you should still respect the danger of her power. Even while having fun, people have lost their lives. MOTHER NATURE'S OCEAN DOES NOT FORGIVE MISTAKES; IT PUNISHES THEM SEVERELY. Disrespect Mother Nature and it could be your last mistake. So again, how can you make a warrior capable of fighting in the salt water? By exposing him to everything.

Among other components of training a SEAL, the US Navy simply exposes them to every obstacle and challenge you can think of. Take all the challenges of the infantry or other land units. Now apply them in the ocean. Six months is just the beginning of how long it takes to integrate all the layers to become a water warrior. A Navy SEAL doesn't deploy with a unit until after three and a half years of training. That's without any hiccups. A student is exposed to a vast number and variety of challenges.

Every SEAL will tell you how their weakness (singular or plural) was/were uncovered and magnified in training. Every single SEAL that has been made was humbled in some way during training. An Olympic swimmer may be found to struggle with dive physics. The fastest runner might struggle in soft sand runs. A good shooter might not be able to hold their breath and swim fifty meters underwater. All these things are woven into pass or fail evolutions that can drop a trainee at any time from training. The reality is a learned humility; no one is good at everything.

Biblical Perspective

> Do not revile the king even in your thoughts, or curse the rich in your bedroom, because a bird in the sky may carry your words, and a bird on the wing may report what you say. (Ecclesiastes 10:20)

> If you show special attention to the man wearing fine clothes and say, "Here's a good seat for you," but say to the poor man, "You stand there" or "Sit on the floor

by my feet," have you not discriminated among yourselves

and become judges with evil thoughts? (James 2:3–4)

Not many of you should become teachers, my fellow believers, because you

know that we who teach will be judged more strictly. We all stumble in many

ways. Anyone who is never at fault in what they say is perfect, able to keep their

whole body in check. When we put bits into the mouths of horses to make them

obey us, we can turn the whole animal. Or take ships as an example—although

they are so large and are driven by strong winds, they are steered by a very small

rudder wherever the pilot wants to go. Likewise, the tongue is a small part of

the body, but it makes great boasts. Consider what a great forest is set on fire by

a small spark. The tongue also is a fire, a world of evil among the parts of the

body. It corrupts the whole body, sets the whole course of one's life on fire, and is

itself set on fire by hell. All kinds of animals, birds, reptiles, and sea creatures

are being tamed and have been tamed by mankind, but no human being can tame

the tongue. It is a restless evil, full of deadly poison. With the tongue, we praise

our Lord and Father, and with it, we curse human beings, who have been made

in God's likeness. (James 3:1–9)

Brothers and sisters, do not slander one another.

Anyone who speaks against a brother or sister or judges

them speaks against the law and judges it. When you

judge the law, you are not keeping it, but sitting in judg-

ment on it. There is only one Lawgiver and Judge, the one

who is able to save and destroy. But you—who are you to

judge your neighbor? (James 4: 11,12)

Don't grumble against one another, brothers and

sisters, or you will be judged. The Judge is standing at the

door. (James 5:9)

Knowing the Bible and especially the book of James is tough on what's in the heart of someone who gossips. Why adhere to the principle if you don't care? Well, this principle, and other biblical character principles, are the most lucrative practices someone can enlist while leading others in this life. Whether you care or not is irrelevant if you believe that the end justifies the means. But if you practice these principles, it will go well with you.

BEFORE YOU JUDGE SOMEONE FOR NOT PER-FORMING HOW YOU'D LIKE THEM TO, CONSIDER THAT EVERY SEAL WARRIOR HAS HIS SHORTCOMINGS. The truth is that some wash out, but all who make it know well they have weaknesses and will admit it. As SEALs, we are not good at everything and we are aware of our shortcomings.

Knowing that, why judge people who fall below elite for not being competent, aware, able, or proficient enough at a certain task? If you want to be a great leader, just help them find their place; you're the boss.

Activation

The application of this matter happens during the side talks at work, around the water cooler or in the break room. Learn to listen for the slander, and before you add your two cents, stop yourself. Instead of thinking about how that person has failed, think about what their strengths are and where they should be placed in the company.

Before you open your mouth and say something derogatory, elevate yourself above the rest and replace that with what they 'should' be doing. Be the kind of leader who empowers people. Nothing builds loyalty more than a leader who cares.

C H A P T E R 1 4

Inspire People to Get Better

Marketplace

I have a good friend who served in the marines. He is substantially larger than me and could easily bench press more than me. I always enjoyed working out with him because we would push each other through the harder reps. He talked a lot of trash, but I always let him know that I could whoop him. Every time his ego got too big, I made sure I let him know that I could take him down. One day he looked at me and said, "Why do you think you can take me?"

I said, "Because you show me your weaknesses. I see them."

After a few days went by, he struck up the question again and he asked, "How do I show you my weakness?"

I said, "You show me your weakness every second of every day as you walk around." Unbeknownst to him, it was his pride.

This completely baffled and enraged him, but he never had the guts to call my bluff and come at me. I simply got in his head. Really, I'm not sure I would've been successful, but I knew that by telling him I could take him, it would turn him into an offensive fighter and thus making his moves very predictable.

Offensive fighters often have their vulnerabilities unguarded. A PREDICTABLE OPPONENT IS ONE THAT THINKS SIM-PLE-MINDEDLY. Offensively or defensively, they are predictable. Because I was unsure if I could actually take him, I wanted to make sure I could predict his moves to be offensive. I crawled in his body and controlled what he would do, how he would feel, and how he would act.

Okay, that's a bit of a stretch, but we're having fun and I want you to realize your potential as a leader. Point is, as a leader, I was able to project some influence on someone else.

I talk with my kids about how advertisements crawl in their bodies and make them think a certain way. It then drags them to the store and forces them to buy something. They disagree this is true, but we have fun talking about it.

There are many ways for leaders to inspire the people who follow them to have fun at work, be happy when they are there and feel good about the work they are doing? How would a leader do that? Think about it.

As a leader, we ignite a passion in people to show up and act however we motivate them. The tools to do this are endless but sometimes we don't know they exist. WE HELP THEM BELIEVE THEY ARE CHANGING THE WORLD. WE ARE POLITE AND GRATEFUL FOR WHAT THEY DO FOR US. WE PAY THEM A GOOD AND FAIR WAGE AND ARE CONCERNED ABOUT THEIR PERSONAL LIVES.

As a leader, you should use whatever you can around you and leverage it to the fullest to keep your people happy in the workplace. Losing that is like taking the nails out of the house. Everything just falls apart.

Military Side

The military has a big problem with morale and reintegration. Recently, the military has a spiked suicide percentage among veterans. No one is certain why it is happening. It's wearing on many people and I believe it's related to people's happiness of employment. Allow me to explain. You see, military leadership is primarily based on fear in the ranks, not morale.

The military doesn't depend on morale to keep enlisted people happy. They don't need to treat the lower echelons well. If you mess up in the military, you will get a dishonorable discharge and a person will deal with it for the rest their life.

This leaves people walking around in an environment motivated, inspired yet still controlled by fear. Some branches of the Department of Defense are better than others. The Air Force treats people much better than the army. I saw this firsthand while I was serving, and you could see it on people's faces. When I went to static line jump school at Fort Benning, Georgia, we stayed on the army base. The young soldiers walked around in fear constantly. Rightly so because I often saw NCOs stop to yell at the younger soldiers for no reason other than they could.

This is different than how officers treated the enlisted men in the SEAL teams. Leaders carry more of a positive attitude and will do everything in their power to help you do your job. Because of the 'special warfare' club we were in, our leadership would very rarely demoralize lower echelon men for doing poorly without first getting the right support from them personally.

Usually, SEAL team leadership would take ownership for the faults of those underneath them. It's a leadership style that I believe works better. Instead of being unproductive, respectful and team orientated leadership styles actually makes people more productive. People are inspired and motivated to come to work and do a good job because they choose to and not because they're afraid of a dishonorable discharge. These are two very opposing methods of motivating employees.

As a private sector leader, you don't have the option of dangling the fear of a dishonorable discharge over someone to motivate them into being productive. Yes, you can fire them, but that won't follow them around in life like a dishonorable discharge does. You also can't rely on a bad economy to scare people to stay at your place of employment. You have to give people another reason to show up and ignite their productivity.

THE MOTIVATION IS YOU, MY GREAT LEADER FRIEND!

Biblical Perspective

There is nothing better on the face of this earth than pure and healthy friendships with close friends. Do you know of someone you can share great, honest, and fun times with absolute trust?

Now, imagine that you are that person and you employ people. Those people coming to work for you enjoy your presence, not because you are "more special" than all the other humans. It's because you are the salt of the earth. Your authenticity plus the fruits of the Spirit are what make you a good person and a good leader. You can only be the change you want to see. You can't force someone to be productive in the workplace, but you can set the example. As Christian leaders, you are watched with double the scrutiny.

> But the fruit of the Spirit is love, joy, peace, for-
> bearance, kindness, goodness, faithfulness, gentleness and
> self-control. (Galatians 5:22)

This isn't manipulating people to work hard because of any reason other than the fact that you lead by example with the Fruit of the Spirit. Lead them well and in a good direction.

Activation

Reflect on some of the missed opportunities you have had to help people. Perhaps you had a bad day, lost your temper a little bit, didn't give credit where credit was due, didn't listen, didn't show appreciation, passed up an act of kindness, or were just downright lazy to interact with your people. Remember, they look to you for inspiration.

Write them down but no need to get anymore mentorship on the subject. You just got it. Don't let those opportunities go without motivating your people. Let the good times roll. You're going to notice a lot of things change. Time to put the nails back into the house! Bring the energy.

CHAPTER 15

The Elephant in the Room

The expression "elephant in the room" or "the elephant in the living room" is a metaphorical phrase an important or enormous topic, problem, or risk that is obvious or that everyone knows about but no one mentions or wants to discuss it. Why? Because it makes at least some of them uncomfortable or is personally, socially, or politically embarrassing, controversial, inflammatory, or dangerous.

If we are willing to overlook something as large and—potentially smelly—as an elephant—we are not leading with integrity or courage.

In my thirty-eight years of existence, I've lived in different places and noticed a difference between people who live on the East Coast and those who live on the West Coast. You see, those who live on the right side will tell you exactly what they think, with words and eye contact. Between New Jersey and Boston, they will even give you a little sauce with it.

Those on the West Coast use their body language and fewer words to make a point. They expect their body language and silence to be just as loud as words. Generally speaking, they might be considered more pacifists by some people.

If someone who grew up on the East Coast was to spend time with someone on the West Coast, they would think this lack of words was really just them being a pacifist. Ask me how I know. I've lived in both places. My experience after growing up in the heart of it all, Ohio, then moving to the West Coast for fourteen years, showed that this is mostly true.

Which are you? Pacifist or not? Some of us are very verbal, but when awkward or difficult situations arise, we shy away. This is not a discussion about introverts and extroverts. THIS IS ABOUT LEADERS WHO MUST COMMUNICATE WITH THEIR FOLLOWERS, EVEN WHEN DIFFICULT TOPICS ARISE.

Most people have been in a situation at work where everyone was wondering about an issue, but no one wanted to talk about it. When people are wondering about those things, it makes for some very suspenseful gatherings. That suspense distracts people mentally and leadership should confront it to regain respect and productivity. Whether you bring the subject up verbally, or with your body language as a pacifist, the topic cannot be ignored; it needs to be addressed. An elephant in the room left unchecked snatches productivity and morale. A leader who deals with the issue gives his people a breath of fresh air and faith in their choice of employment.

Marketplace

Elon Musk has been one to make headlines for having made huge feats in the past two decades. He has also made headlines for saying unnecessary things. If I were to put my finger to the wind, I would say he is 70 percent a madly motivated entrepreneur, 10 percent scientist, and 20 percent leader.

In 2018, the board of his electric car company, Tesla, has changed policy to reign in his Twitter account. This is because he created volatility in the shareholders' stock price. For many months and years, the elephant in the room of the board meetings was his public perception of temperament.

The situation caused distraction among the executives and the volatility continued. No one wanted to bring the matter up with their boss and he should've confronted the elephant with a bit of humility. The board should've worked together with him to create a solution.

It's an easy situation to fix. All he needed to do is get a few people's advice and approval before posting things on Twitter.

Problem solved and move on, but the elephant in the room grew because of leadership ego.

Military Side

I assure you that if a leader were to have a pacifist attitude in the SEAL teams, they and their whole team would be dead. Let's just take the leadership away and just focus on the team; hard discussions need to happen. Can you imagine if you're about to go into battle and you see that your soldier doesn't have batteries in his night vision? That's a mistake that could kill everyone. What if your employee isn't taking their job seriously? What if the break room is constantly a place of drama?

Let's say the elephant in the room isn't a big deal. It's low on the Richter scale of importance. Do you still address it? Absolutely yes! Don't miss the point here. The reason you confront the elephant in the room is to show people you're a leader and will keep the environment safe from uncertainty.

If you choose the easy road, you're not a leader.

Biblical Perspective

As a leader of followers, people want to work for a well-oiled machine. People like to take pride in their companies. I would suggest it's important to get ahead of the little details people worry about. Even a small drop of poison can fill the whole pond. Jesus teaches that even a little yeast can work its way all through the dough.

When they went across the lake, the disciples forgot to take bread. "Be careful," Jesus said to them. "Be on your guard against the yeast of the Pharisees and Sadducees." They discussed this among themselves and said, "It is because we didn't bring any bread." Aware of their discussion, Jesus asked, "You of little faith, why are you talking among yourselves about having no bread?

Do you still not understand? Don't you remember the five loaves for the five thousand, and how many basketfuls you gathered? Or the seven loaves for the four thousand, and how many basketfuls you gathered? How is it you don't understand that I was not talking to you about bread? But be on your guard against the yeast of the Pharisees and Sadducees." Then they understood that he was not telling them to guard against the yeast used in bread, but against the teaching of the Pharisees and Sadducees. (Matthew 16:5)

I WOULD SUGGEST THAT AS LEADERS, WE ALLOW PEOPLE THE PEACE OF MIND TO NOT THINK ABOUT THE DETAILS WE ARE TOO SCARED TO ENCOUNTER ON OUR BEHALF. IT REALLY ISN'T CONSIDERATE TO THEM.

Maybe one of the reasons we don't engage the elephant in the room is fear. We are afraid of the task or the outcome. If that is the case, fear is the yeast. Only a little bit of fear holds you back from displaying a big lesson in leadership within yourself.

The story of Mary and Martha in the Bible was a mini display of this large principle for us to see.

As Jesus and his disciples were on their way, he came to a village where a woman named Martha opened her home to him. She had a sister called Mary, who sat at the Lord's feet listening to what he said. But Martha was distracted by all the preparations that had to be made. She came to him and asked, "Lord, don't you care that my sister left me to do the work by myself? Tell her to help me!" (Luke 10:38–42)

Can you feel the atmosphere shift with that sharp demand? In that moment, everyone would have been uneasy and the elephant in the room grew larger. But Jesus, being the good leader he was, confronted it and shifted the atmosphere again.

"Martha, Martha," the Lord answered, "you are worried and upset about many things, but few things are needed—or indeed only one. Mary has chosen what is better, and it will not be taken away from her."

Jesus confronted Martha and said her sister was the one doing the right thing. Mary was using her window of opportunity to learn better than Martha. But we tend to let the many Marthas go without confronting them in our world.

Don't let the Marthas or situations in your people poison the pond. Keep things clean and lighthearted for the sake of your cause!

Activation

I want you to make a list of five of the issues you have avoided in your life—questions people have about the company or you. All these issues are time bombs. Prioritize them in a serious manner as to resolve the issue completely so that you don't have to talk about it again.

If you can't think of five things, ask around and I'm sure honest people will tell you.

CHAPTER 16

Managers Versus Leaders—Pick Your Path

This capitalist economy you and I live in holds as many different kinds of leaders as there are colors in the rainbow. Managers, executives, entrepreneurs, tour guides, teachers, coaches, and religious heads of churches—all of them have their leadership skill set.

As a company grows, it enters and exits different stages much like a growing human going through different growth stages. We are born at about seven pounds and completely helpless. As we grow and learn how to use our "getaway sticks" (what we call legs in special warfare), we take falls and get bumps and scrapes.

Then there's puberty, acne, cliques at school, and at the age eighteen, we are considered an "adult." This word, "adult," is so loosely used. I would say you are not an adult measured by years but by maturity. Some reach adulthood by the age fourteen, some by forty-four. PAYING RENT, HOLDING A JOB, OR HAVING KIDS IS BY NO MEANS A MEASUREMENT OF ADULTHOOD.

In comparison, a company has its birth, has its toddler years where it makes mistakes, and falls a few times. It goes through its puberty years, and depending on the leadership, it will hit adulthood when it has matured. Having a good number of employees, a marketing plan, and a strong company presence is by no means a measure of a mature company. Company maturity is measured by intangibles.

Do you trust in your company? Much like you can look at a person and know if they are mature or not, so you can with a company. THERE IS A GUT FEELING IN ALL OF US ABOUT OUR PLACE OF WORK. YOU KNOW IN YOUR GUT IF SOMETHING IS RIGHT OR NOT, ESPECIALLY THE EMPLOYEES. Now I could tangibly measure company maturity against paying down debt, liquid reserves ready to put out fires, or take opportunities and also with a good twenty-year plan.

Marketplace

Forget the kind of group someone leads and let's talk about the skill sets required in each of the growth periods for a moment.

First, the baby phase. Some are good at starting a company, getting it off the ground, and creating a presence. You can YouTube, Google, and Bing an outline about how to easily do this. This takes a good measure of endurance, belief in yourself, and charisma to get others to follow. At the same time, you will probably not take much of an income from your business, so you can do other things with your money. You have to have the patience and faith that you'll be paid when you exit or pay yourself well if you stay for the long term.

Second, the toddler phase. You have a company with all the framework in place. Typically, this is a company with three to five employees and is ready to expand. Some leaders are good at coming in, hiring people, and moving it through the stages of adolescence and puberty. Just like starting a company, this takes endurance, belief in yourself, and charisma, but you also need to be able to take risks. The largest limiting factor between leaders who are good at starting companies and leaders who are good at growing companies is risk.

To grow a company from three to three hundred people, you need to hang it out there. For example, the worst-case scenario is you may have to hire people before you have the money to pay people. You may have to hold paychecks a few days or pay insufficient fund penalties to your bank in this period because you're taking risks. You may have to go to the bank and borrow at a high rate to fund your plan. Yet that's exactly the person you need to be to grow a company.

Thirdly, the young adult phase. You have a fifty-plus-person company that's ready to head into maturity. This is when you hire a seasoned CEO or president to run the company. This person needs hindsight and foresight added to his resumé of leadership characteristics to build a big company. Putting people into place, pay down debt, and write a twenty-year plan.

Military Side

Unfortunately, not all of the military side examples are public relations for the military. There is a clash between the two cultures. Each side, military and civilian, produces different kinds of leadership. This reveals the biggest difference between military and corporate leaders. Military leaders are given charge of a group of soldiers. IN MILITARY LEADERSHIP, THERE IS NO NEED FOR GROWTH WISDOM AND TWENTY-YEAR VISION PLANS. GROWING YOUR UNIT IS OF NO CONCERN. This is one of the big reasons transition to the marketplace is difficult for DOD members.

Military leaders do not have to possess all the characteristics of a marketplace leader. Marketing and accounting knowledge are few things that don't need to be on the list. Some things that are on the list are the presence of your person among your men. Intellect for the mission. The ability to develop and achieve your mission along with high personal character for men to follow are all well-known as well as vital.

This is an unspoken elephant in the room. It's true that military veterans are mostly not prepared for the corporate world in this particular aspect concerning growth in a group. It's offensive to someone who has led many men in battle to hear they aren't ready to lead people in the marketplace.

Hopefully, to you as a leader in the marketplace, this helps you hire and put vets in a position they are good at and can use their strengths outside of the military. Hopefully, you can help train them in the tools of growing their group and help them reintegrate in an effective manner.

My question to you is, Which level are you good at? Where is your niche? It's very important that you know yourself that well.

If you want to start a company, be careful that you have the endurance to wait three years before you're ready to reap the success. You might be better off waiting for a while until the company is established before you go in there and buy it. If you purchase a small company then you need to know how to grow it. If you don't know this, you have no business taking something over. You would be better off grabbing a fishing pole and go throw a hook in the water.

The important lesson here is to know who you are and place yourself where your strengths can be magnified. Trying to fill the shoes of a position that you're not wired for is like trying to pass a square through a round hole. It just doesn't work.

Was Muhammad Ali a good basketball player? The answer is who knows? He was a talented fighter and that's how he excelled. You will excel at the things you're wired for. If you want to move up a level, learn your weaknesses and work on them relentlessly to become a higher-level leader.

Biblical Perspective

There is not much difference in your daily activities between the different levels of leadership, but at the same time, it's a huge difference between the two. Being the better leader requires huge steps that only take you small increments.

Going from one level to the next is like the difference of a tenth of a second in a hundred-meter dash.

Now faith is confidence in what we hope for and assurance about what we do not see. (Hebrews 11:1)

Going to the next level requires more faith, but not much else once your professional character is interwoven. So, as they say, another level, another devil. The higher you go up the mountain of faith, the lonelier it gets. The less people can relate to you, the more people will judge you. It's just like only Moses who could go up to get the Ten Commandments, so too you must be able to be one in a thousand when it comes to character and faith as a leader.

Faith in your ability to achieve success is the difference in what you choose to pursue and why.

As a man thinks in his heart, so is he. (Proverbs 23:7)

Activation

Answer these questions internally and find what you need to work on to go to the next level:

Are you a manager or a leader?

Are you good at taking orders from a leader and carrying out a task?

Are you a leader who understands how to delegate tasks to capable managers to grow a company?

Then answer why you're good at that level?

How do you grow your knowledge and become a better leader at each level?

Would you rather start a company, take a company over and grow it, or bring a twenty-year plan to a company?

Do you trust God? Do you trust yourself? Ponder your answers the rest of the day.

CHAPTER 17

Listen Like a Leader

Today's politics in our great America is a joke to the rest of the world. Our Congress and Senate argue with each other like middle school kids on the playground. Gossiping, contradicting, making fun of people, and finding skeletons in their closet only to air them out in public. Defaming other Americans has become a political tool for gaining a seat in office.

On the other hand, (silent pause for emphasis), WHAT IT TAKES TO BE A GOOD RESPECTED LEADER HAS BECOME THE OPPOSITE OF WHAT IT TAKES TO GET ELECTED TO PUBLIC OFFICE. Being elected isn't to be confused with being a respected leader. One huge part of being a respected leader is being a good listener.

If you're like me, you carry a ton of ideas and visions around with you. Carrying ideas around with you also comes the urge to tell others about them. Yet listening is what wins people over. I've had to learn that "people don't care what you know until they know you care." When they know you care, they're ready to hear what you have to say.

Today I would like you to consider an element of listening that has for the most part gone unspoken. Maybe you've heard in the past people suggest that listening has mostly to do with eye contact and body language while someone else is talking. Restating what they told you is a plus for further communication acknowledgment. All that is great and shows a willingness to listen, but today consider the top tier of listening to someone.

Check it, first and foremost, totally disregard your opinion about the matter and apply yourself to thinking about their position. Put yourself in their shoes, think of yourself with their color of skin. Think about things from their perspective. Most importantly consider yourself wrong about the subject while considering they are right. Throw off all previous knowledge you think you have on the subject and allow yourself to hear them out.

What happens is a whole new dimension of communication that leaders need to utilize, especially politicians. You'll enter into someone else's world. You'll enter their perspective, in their body, using their eyes. Even while debating the two big no-no's with friends and family, religion, and politics, you'll find much success.

Now stop right there! I didn't say to allow yourself to be persuaded by their opinion. Not at all! I said to listen to them. REAL UNDERSTANDING AND KNOWLEDGE CAN BE DERIVED FROM OTHERS AND ADDED TO YOUR LEARNING. If you hold on to your own beliefs and presumptions about life, business, and politics, you are limiting yourself.

Marketplace

This is the difference between being the president and being a senator. A senator debates a topic from his side of the aisle. While someone else is talking, they may have their eye contact and body language engaged but they are ready to reply with a right jab and left hook. No transfer of information has really taken place and no understanding has been gained by that senator. Just a waste of time, breath, and words.

Now to be presidential is to hear multiple people and make a decision about the best direction to go in. Listening to all sides is crucial for the top decision-maker to go in the best direction.

So, which are you? A senator or the president? Do you argue back and forth with people, or do you take in all the information and gain understanding?

Listen, true learning and gaining understanding is a big barrier people place in front of themselves without knowing it. It takes a big drop in your pride to listen. You have to disrobe your ego and humble yourself like a child trying to eagerly learn about the world.

Military Side

Serving as a part of the most lethal units in the world has been one of the highest honors of my life. Yet make no mistake that TO MAKE IT INTO BIG BOYS' CLUB, YOU MUST LEARN TO LISTEN AND LEAVE YOUR EGO BEHIND. Let me say it differently: you will be kicked out if your ego goes unchecked. A large ego makes you dangerous. In a profession like special warfare, you must allow others to give you advice. A big ego leads to a "do it on my own" attitude. That leads to complacency, and complacency kills.

To train for the teams we practiced many kinds of diving and did our best to perfect them all. Before every tactical combat dive we did, we would have a dive supervisor check. A "sup check" is conducted right before you enter the water by someone qualified to do so. With all the different systems we took into the water with us, it was important to have correctly donned the gear so that it properly works underwater.

Yes, we were knowledgeable about the items we dove with, but we all make mistakes. The check was to make sure we had everything in working order. Are the air tanks on? Do any straps overlap? Is our depth gauge zeroed? Knife strapped on? Weapons? Systems on? Mask and fins ready? Dry suit sealed? Everything was to be systematically checked. Sure, we mostly had things right, but mistakes are often made.

It all has to be in perfect working order before you enter the water. The risk is mission failure or death. Any correction given is received with sincere gratefulness. What's at stake is life and death, especially when operating under the sea.

Same principle goes during all training. It takes great humility and an ability to absorb what you must to be the best.

Why do we think it is any different when trying to be the best leader possible? Do we think lowering our ego will be perceived as weakness to others? Do we think it's important to trick people into thinking you have all the right answers already? Being the best takes curiosity for knowledge, and if we don't throw off what you know, our learning will cease.

Mark Twain said, **"What gets us into the most trouble is not what we do not know. What gets us in trouble is what we know for certain to be true that, turns out not to be true."**

Believe me. Listening with intent will catapult you to the top of any group.

Biblical Perspective

So, dig down deep into your soul. What would the reason be that someone doesn't listen? What are the barriers to listening? When you find the answer to your resistance, I bet you also find another reason to practice some good old-fashioned sanctification. You know, that thing that happens when you find out you're not perfect. When that's paired with "the fear of the Lord," transformation can happen.

My dear brothers and sisters, take note of this: Everyone should be quick to listen, slow to speak and slow to become angry. (James 1:19)

Okay, a New Testament commandment to listen and not speak. We should put that in our pocket as a believer. But then our friend in the Lord, the apostle Paul, wrote a letter to the Corinthians. That describes, what I believe, to be a mirrored listening trait in chapter

12. He talked about spiritual gifts. The list of spiritual gifts looks like this:

Wisdom, Knowledge, Prophecy, Healing, Miraculous power, Distinguishing between spirits, Speaking in tongues and Interpreting tongues.

Okay, so great, but what does this have to do with this principle of listening? It's all in the ending of the chapter, you see, then Paul gives us a little secret:

Now eagerly desire the greater gifts. And yet I will show you the most excellent way. (1 Corinthians 12:31)

What's this most excellent way? Love.

If I do not have love, I gain nothing. (1 Corinthians 13:3)

Verse 1 says, "You are only a resounding gong without love."

What he is saying is that love trumps the entire list of manifestations! It is an incredible statement if you really ponder it! And he says that if you don't have love, you cannot "fully know." In this interesting word "fully know," Paul links it to love.

So how will you show love and attempt to fully know anything about life under the sun if you don't listen? LISTENING REALLY COMES OUT OF LOVE.

It is a decision you must make in your core to listen when your followers speak to you. It shows love on the most basic and primal levels.

What most humans do in a conversation is decide before someone talks as to whether they will accept or reject what the other person has to say. That or you decide that you are more intelligent than the other person.

Again, a decision you must make in your spirit before you speak with someone else that you are humble enough to consider them knowledgeable and valuable as a child of God to be respected and listened to.

Activation

Today I have three tasks for you. I want you to ask three different people three different questions. First ask someone about why they believe in their faith; listen as though they are fully right.

Second, ask someone why they choose to belong to a political party and apply the same listening.

Third, ask someone who looks fit what you should do to get in shape.

Today's drill isn't for you to convert to a faith. Vote like some-

one else or get fit. It's to learn how to learn and discern like a true

leader. The barriers inside of you need to fall, and this is practice.

CHAPTER 18

Don't Put Others in Jail

As a father of four small, beautiful children, I am becoming a subject matter expert in conflict resolution. Conflicts can arise at the drop of a hat. Literally. One of the boys drops one of the girls' hat on the ground, and *poof!* a conflict has arrived. I can almost set my watch till the next conflict comes, and Lord help us if they haven't eaten and they are a little hungry.

Most of the time the older one gets the upper hand over the smaller one, whether it's over a toy or a swing or you name it. What happens without adults to come and help resolve the conflict is the little ones will most likely shut down and pout while the other plays gleefully.

I've taught my children (at least I hope I have) that one who puts the younger kids' heart in jail has to go take it out of jail. It's their job to take the younger sibling and restore them to a happy heart. It's very powerful when this situation happens in the younger one and it's a good life principle most adults have never learned.

All of us are born with complete self-focus and we get less than one hundred years to figure out how to share our earth with others. SOME OF US DON'T KNOW HOW TO RESOLVE A CONFLICT AND WE ARE ACTING OUT FIVE-YEAR-OLD CONFLICTS AT FORTY-FIVE YEARS OLD. It looks like this.

You get offended somehow and you use a simple truth negatively as a verbal dagger on someone else. Then you allow it to linger unresolved, thus offending someone else and putting their heart in jail. If this is you, let me just say how easy it is to take the other person out of jail. AN HONEST BUT DIFFICULT THIRTY-SEC-OND CONVERSATION, COMBINED WITH A HANDFUL OF HUMILITY, AND IT'S OVER. Most of the people in our world don't care about the emotional well-being of people we are upset with. We might even feel they deserve it deep down in our subconscious.

As silly as this lesson may sound, as a leader, it's very easy to put someone's heart in jail and create for yourself a time bomb in the future. You may be able to raise your voice, condemn, judge, or sneer without pushback in the moment. Or so one might think. Yet at the same time, you just set a time bomb to explode at a later date in the future, ready to tear down what you've built and build a bad reputation in its place.

IN THE PRESENT, DO YOU KNOW THAT YOUR EMPLOYEE ISN'T THINKING ABOUT THEIR JOB, BUT THEY ARE MOST LIKELY REPLAYING WHAT YOU HAVE SAID IN THEIR HEAD? They will be spending time on outside thoughts, not their job. They might polish their resumé while on the clock or search for jobs at their desk.

Marketplace

As we talk about putting someone's heart in jail, let me ask you this: who was better, Michael Jordan or Lebron James? A loaded question that's been debated before. Let's think about it this way. Michael had a way of embarrassing his defender. He would tell them what he was about to do to them, and then he would do exactly that. Thing is, he gained the respect of his opponents, made things fun, and played with a friendly zeal. People wanted to share the court with him, both on his team and against. He had a gravitational aura that simply attracted people to him.

LeBron has a way of playing hard for a win, but don't get in his way. Some of his teammates have said in the past that playing with him was felt like walking on eggshells. If the team lost the game, the blame is on them, whether he said it or not. People didn't want to be on the court with him because some have felt that he plays with a hostile zeal. People aren't excited to play with him because they have an unspoken fear of being thrown under a bus.

So, which one are you as a leader? LeBron or Michael? Do people like working with you? Do you play with a fun zeal or an angry zeal? Another marketplace example: when my gym was being threatened by the city building code officers with a hefty fee for relocating within my building complex. It was stressful. The requirements were unattainable. I had four children to support and wasn't sure if the city would allow my business to remain.

One day when the code enforcement officer came to my business for a walk-through, I could tell he was a bit tense. He knew what his enforcement meant for me, and I'm sure he expected a negative reaction from me. Maybe he was familiar with emotions people get when told to shut down. I decided to take him out of that prison and make his day better. So, I thanked him for his civil service much like someone does when they thank a soldier.

I even quoted to him a verse in the Bible I had just read that morning, Deuteronomy 22:8 (NIV): "When you build a new house, make a parapet around your roof so that you may not bring the guilt of bloodshed on your house if someone falls from the roof." I explained to him that he was helping save lives and I appreciated that cause.

His demeanor completely changed, and I believe in that moment, he stopped working against me and started thinking about how to help me. I essentially took his heart out of jail. I'm sure instead of going back to the office and talking about a difficult conversation he had with me to his coworkers, he went back and asked how his team can end a senseless rule.

YOU SEE, A LEADER DOESN'T CARE ABOUT THE BAD NEWS. HE CARES ABOUT THE BEARER OF BAD NEWS.

I want you to be able to step out of the old reality and excel as a leader! It's important that you know how to take another person's heart out of jail. As this may sound as a new concept, it's important as a leader to know how to build trust and get feedback on the most difficult issues.

Biblical Perspective

To the elders among you, I appeal as a fellow elder and a witness of Christ's sufferings who also will share in the glory to be revealed: Be shepherds of God's flock that is under your care, watching over them—not because you must, but because you are willing, as God wants you to be; not pursuing dishonest gain, but eager to serve; not lording it over those entrusted to you, but being examples to the flock. And when the Chief Shepherd appears, you will receive the crown of glory that will never fade away. (1 Peter 5:1–4)

As a leader, I can see the potential you have to lead people in a good direction or lead them in a bad direction. As the owner of a company, manager of the department, CEO, pastor, or whatever, people follow you and they will usually put up with your time bombs for a little while. Reason being is because you are a leader and they are following you. But you should actively be uprooting any time bomb around. Why?

Let no debt remain outstanding, except the continuing debt to love one another, for whoever loves others has fulfilled the law. (Romans 13:8)

Some of us allow unresolved offenses to linger. In that case, I suggest practicing something I call reverse forgiveness. REVERSE

FORGIVENESS IS NOT YOU FORGIVING SOMEONE ELSE BUT YOU ASKING SOMEONE TO FORGIVE YOU. If someone has unforgiveness in their heart, it is in a jail cell and they are in sin. If they don't follow Jesus, they don't know how to get out. Forgiveness is the ultimate professional tool that will keep your Waze steady and solid. Practicing a reverse forgiveness means if you create an offense, you go to that person and admit you were wrong and apologize for it. You didn't ask them to forgive you. This is fulfilling Romans 13:8.

We have all heard the story of Jonah, about how he was swallowed by a big fish and brought to where he was supposed to go anyway. For my entire childhood, I thought that if I disobeyed the Lord I'd be swallowed by a whale. But the story doesn't end there. You see, after he finishes his mission to the people of Nineveh and they repented, he gets angry with the Lord and starts pouting because he felt they still deserved destruction. Let's read starting chapter 4.

But to Jonah this seemed very wrong, and he became angry. He prayed to the Lord, "Isn't this what I said, Lord, when I was still at home? That is what I tried to forestall by fleeing to Tarshish. I knew that you are a gracious and compassionate God, slow to anger and abounding in love, a God who relents from sending calamity. Now, Lord, take away my life, for it is better for me to die than to live."

But the Lord replied, "Is it right for you to be angry?" Jonah had gone out and sat down at a place east of the city. There he made himself a shelter, sat in its shade and waited to see what would happen to the city. Then the Lord God provided a leafy plant and made it grow up over Jonah to give shade for his head to ease his discomfort, and Jonah was very happy about the plant. But at dawn the next day God provided a worm, which chewed the plant so that it withered. When the sun rose, God provided a scorching east wind, and the sun blazed on Jonah's head so that he grew faint. He wanted to die, and said, "It would be better for me to die than to live."

But God said to Jonah, "Is it right for you to be angry about the plant?"

"It is," he said. "And I'm so angry I wish I were dead."

But the Lord said, "You have been concerned about this plant, though you did not tend it or make it grow. It sprang up overnight and died overnight. And should I not have concern for the great city of Nineveh, in which there are more than a hundred and twenty thousand people who cannot tell their right hand from their left—and also many animals?"

Jonah cared more about his shade than the people who were about to face judgment in the city of Nineveh. After reading that you might think Jonah is so selfish and the people in Nineveh who didn't know the Lord in the first place didn't deserve destruction as the Lord thought. But just like Jonah, how much more do we not care about the destruction of someone's emotional well-being if we don't alleviate their anger or offense because it doesn't affect us? If we are not in jail, and someone else is, we should care about them as if we are them.

REVERSE FORGIVENESS SIMPLIFIED: YOU BRING THE MATTER UP AND CREATE AN ATMOSPHERE WHERE OTHERS CAN FORGIVE YOU. This keeps the devil from getting a foothold and you from growing a time bomb.

Example: "I did this. It was wrong. Can you forgive me?"

Activation

Do you put others' hearts in jail around you or keep them free? To find out, ask someone in the leadership above you because Lord knows they already see it. Did you think you were hiding it from the experienced? They will most likely have other advice for you as well to help you with the necessary surgery you're about to do on your personality and character.

Your boss may be waiting for you to mature before he promotes you. This will show him you're ready to advance. You see, working on your character does the opposite of a time bomb. Working on character builds your reputation as well as the confidence of the group you're leading.

CHAPTER 19

Build Karma. It Will Always Come Back to You

Karma is defined as building up goodwill in your current life that will come back to you later in life. Although I'm not Buddhist, there seems to be a thread of this principle through most faiths on earth. As a young person, I did not believe in karma and definitely wasn't of the mindset that little things mattered. But through the years, I have seen this principal work. It seems that most things you do will come back to you, good and bad.

In the Holy Bible, it says, "Do not judge, or you too will be judged. For in the same way you judge others, you will be judged, and with the measure you use, it will be measured to you" (Matthew 7:1–2).

In the Muslim Quran, it is said that your good deeds and your prayers build a bridge over hell where there is the lake of burning fire. If you build enough bricks (good deeds), your bridge will allow you access to heaven.

Those who don't believe in a God have the "universe." I would suggest for your consideration that even most atheists and agnostics believe something along the lines of "do good deeds inside of the universe and the universe will pay it back to you."

For now, let's just call this building of good deeds by the Buddhist term karma. For someone like yourself who is focused on self-development and character, karma is a valuable tool. I suggest it's even better when your good deeds are unseen or kept private. Otherwise, you run the risk of exploitation, and that has the opposite effect of karma. You'll be admonished for drawing attention to the good things you do.

PRACTICING GOOD DEEDS WITHOUT BEING SEEN CREATES A HABIT OF DOING GOOD DEEDS IN GENERAL. You will look for opportunities to fix this world around us, from which you'll build a reputation.

Marketplace

I knew a man who was the head of a large corporation and conducted many job interviews to hire people for the management level. He had an interesting trick on judging someone's character. He would place a notepad on the floor near the chair where the applicant was going to sit. He made sure it was in plain sight and awkwardly out of place. What the applicant did with that notepad determined how they would be considered for the job.

If they disregarded the notepad completely, they would be disregarded for the job completely. If they picked it up and put it in a place of organization, they would be put in his organization. Simple enough of a trick. But when you consider that it came from a wise elderly man, you have to conclude he has found extreme power in an honest individual's triumphs over their talent.

The real value of building karma is the practice that good deeds builds good habits. Just like working out muscles makes them stronger. If you build an identity like that, people will come to know you and your good identity. This will ultimately help prevent future time bombs that threaten what you've built and build a bad reputation. If you think there's no value in practicing small deeds, you're wrong and probably nearsighted. If you ever have a bad day, people will come to you, and help you. Although it may take a few years, maybe decades, it will come back to you.

You can build all day long every day with little things. Picking up a loose piece of trash. If you ding someone's car in the parking lot, you write a letter of apology and your contact information and a leader after God's own heart leave it on their windshield. Hold the door open for the elderly. Say "Thank you" and "Excuse me" without fail, even when you don't think it's necessary.

This is especially a big deal now because there are lots of industries that rely on service and for the most part people think their "Thank you" comes in the form of money. There is a famous saying that if you want to know a person's character, watch how they treat a waiter or salesclerk or anyone below their social position.

As a prior elite military member, the principles are virtually the same as any profession in the rest of the world. Building karma in the job you do will increase self-preservation. Doing the small things well also helps build karma. Helping your teammate with tasks and paying attention to small details will ensure a successful mission... and a longer life.

Military Side

As a soldier who served in a war, you may have asked this question. "If you kill someone on the battlefield, will it build bad karma, create PTSD, and come back to haunt me in some way?" I would return the question this way: "What's worse, refusing to follow orders or doing your job and fighting as a team?" Maybe pulling the trigger saves lives. When a force like ours shows up on scene, there's a reason we are there. Period. We are going to make the world safer.

Just like cops are forced to pull their guns and do their job, so are we. Yet the building of karma in the military professionally will follow you outside of your service and precede you wherever you go. So practicing good habits will build good karma to follow you elsewhere.

Now let's build on what we know so far and explore the opposite of karma. What does it look like to build bad karma? Have you ever noticed the suck-up who is always doing good things in full view of their boss? That's *instant* bad karma in many ways. How about road rage? Pushing your way through a crowd. Walking past a piece of trash. Acting like you didn't see someone to hold the door open for them. These all build bad karma and rob you of opportunities to mold good habits, not to mention a good reputation.

Yes, good habits need to be worked at. Have you ever heard someone say, "That person is very difficult to work with," speaking about one of their coworkers? When you do not show loyalty to the absent and talk behind people's backs, you destroy your own credibility and build the opposite of karma. Seriously, you will give yourself away more than you know if you don't practice good character, repulsing other people, the effects of which are worse for leaders.

As a leader, how do you know when someone is brownnosing you or if you are simply in front of a highly excited employee? A question every leader who has been humbled should ask themselves. I got to witness this firsthand, the hard way.

I was a part of an organization that turned against the head of the company. Everything he had built over two decades and worked for turned against him in a day.

I remember sitting with him over coffee hearing him say how incredible it was that for twenty or more years people looked up to him and we're very nice to him when he was in charge, but when he was asked to leave, people wouldn't return his phone calls or give him the time of day. They wouldn't even talk to him in public.

He said he wished he would have recognized this while he was leading because it would've changed the decisions he made. Often people treat those above them a lot better than they treat those below them.

Today I'd like to share with you a piece of knowledge I learned from that situation. When you're in leadership, I encourage you to look at how your employees treat those who are underneath them. HOW PEOPLE ACT IN THE PROFESSIONAL WORLD ISN'T EXACTLY A REFLECTION OF THEIR CHARACTER, BUT HOW THEY TREAT THOSE UNDERNEATH THEM IS. So when you're in the lunchroom, watch with a careful eye. Learn to watch people closer when you look away than when you're looking at them.

As for you my 'good leader' friend, build karma at all times. It will help you build good habits that will one day come back to you.

Biblical Perspective

My father is a great man of God. I remember often I would walk into his bedroom to ask him a question and would find him kneeling at his bedside, hands folded and a bowed head talking to God Almighty. He was a prayer warrior, more so than I'll ever know. When I got married, he quoted Ralph Waldo Emerson during the ceremony that I'd like to share:

SOW A THOUGHT, REAP AN ACTION. SOW AN ACTION, REAP A HABIT. SOW A HABIT, REAP A CHARACTER. SOW A CHARACTER, REAP A DESTINY.

So you can see that just simply practicing good habits starts in the mind and ends with developing good habits. This principle is sprinkled all over the Old and New testaments.

As I have observed, those who plow evil and those who sow trouble reap it. (Job 4:8)

Blessed is the one who does not walk in step with the wicked or stand in the way that sinners take or sit in the company of mockers, but whose delight is in the law of the Lord, and who meditates on his law day and night—whatever they do prospers. (Psalm 1:1–3)

So in everything, do to others what you would have them do to you, for this sums up the Law and the Prophets. (Matthew 7:12)

"Put your sword back in its place," Jesus said to him, "for all who draw the sword will die by the sword. (Matthew 26:52)

Alexander the metalworker did me a great deal of harm. The Lord will repay him for what he has done. (2 Timothy 2:14)

Christian karma is God watching over those who practice good deeds and they do what is right even when it hurts.

Activation

I hope over time you'll see the value of building good habits that can build a good reputation. For starters, here are a few things you can try today.

Let's resurrect chivalry in any way possible. Don't walk past trash in any place that you care about. Your work, your house, or your place of worship. Stop, bend down, and snatch that sucker up. I bet when you dispose of that tiny piece of garbage, a small smile will come on your face.

Offer generously your time to people who need help with projects around their house or moving. Sometimes people will take advantage of you, but it will always come back to you in the end. Someway, somehow, sometime in the future. And always treat those under you better than you treat those over you!

CHAPTER 20

Encourage Mentorship

All of us come to a point in life when it comes time to make an important decision. You've come to a fork in the road and now you have to choose left or right. It takes a long time and you may have sought out advice from those you respect.

Mentorship is so crucial to us because others have gone before us and they have golden nuggets that we need. You know, mentorship simplified is just the download of information. Honestly, college simplified is mentorship of many micro topics to help you later in your professional career.

Well, did you know you make about sixty thousand decisions every day? Did you seek mentorship in those? No. But you made it and did just fine, didn't you? In this chapter I want you to see the value of seeking advice without the all too often side effect of becoming a sheep or puppet.

I want you to be your own person. When you do, you'll be half a leader. You'll be a full leader when you start mentoring other people and presenting them the freedom to make their own decisions. **MENTORING OTHERS IS A SOBERING RESPONSIBILITY YOU SHOULD STEWARD WITH CAREFUL DILIGENCE AND A HUMBLE HEART.**

Marketplace

If you are a small business owner, there are, usually, local groups of experienced leaders who can give you round table advice.

A friend of mine wanted to start a painting business. He was a very good painter but knew nothing about the nuts and bolts of starting a business. He went to a community round table and found a guy who had owned a painting business for thirty years. They met one-on-one and the man explained all the details on how to run a successful operation.

You should have seen the big fat smile he wore for a week. He was charged and electrified about his gained knowledge. He was no longer stressing about hiring employees, filing taxes, or sending people on a job while he wasn't there. He was empowered by a mentor. Since then he has opened his business, has three full-time crews, and is usually booked out two months in advance, all because of a mentor.

Military Side

As a military officer, you are usually required to have a mentor. "Required" is the word to use. Officers are given the grave responsibility to lead other men and tell them what to do. So seeking mentorship for decision making is an admirable thing to do.

We all have traumatic times in life that stay with us. It's like that traumatic memory is a blink away and you're right back in the same experience. I can remember a few decisions I had to face back as a senior in high school. I knew I wanted to join the service to challenge myself to find out what I was made of. So I made my rounds to recruiters from all four branches of the services.

Looking back on myself, I was self-searching. For some reason, I just had to find out who I was. So my search was on for the hardest challenge the military had to offer.

After I had met with all of them, I decided to try out for the Navy SEALs. When I heard about the hell week challenge they had, I knew that was it. I knew that if I didn't attempt the challenge, I would have always wondered if I would have ever been able to do it.

When I told my friends about the challenge I wanted to take, they laughed at me and said I would never make it. They said, "You don't have the right mentality for that."

My mom said, "You're going to have to face failure at a young age, that's too bad."

My father said, "No boy of mine is going into the military. Tell me what college you want to go to, and I'll pay for it." It was obvious he didn't believe in me.

So I said "See ya" to all of the people who offered their advice. My mind was the only thing that told me to "go." There was nothing that would stop me from trying. Little did I know that's all I needed. With all the conversations I had, I got not one piece of positive advice or encouragement. Yet those words molded me more than any mentorship or wise advice could. For some reason, every time someone told me I couldn't do it just made me want it more.

Then when my time came to reenlist, I had fulfilled my six years of service, I weighed the thought of getting out of the military, and my fellow warriors advised me to stay in. They explained that all my hard work to get to where I was in the service would be lost and I wouldn't be able to return to that same spot. But I didn't follow their advice and followed my gut and took the risk of starting a family outside of the military's safety net.

After a few years of working a steady, good-paying job, I decided to start a CrossFit gym. Not one person said that was a good idea and it "wasn't a real job," but that's what I did, and it went well for me. Again, I didn't take action on their advice and I learned a ton about business and people.

Then I chose to sell my house and my gym to travel with my family in an RV. Only one person said that was a good idea—my brother. Everyone else said to stay and work hard because I wouldn't be able to make up the lost finances. But again, I followed my gut.

I would not be where I am today had I not followed my gut in every major decision I've had. The point in all of this is to take advice, but the choice is still yours.

Remember those sixty thousand decisions you make every day? What's the difference between a small decision and a big decision?

Both decisions have in common that they are yours to make, not your mentors. Your life is amazingly your own. Don't limit mentorship to a single conversation; use your eyes and ears at all times. Take it all in, consider it, and discard the bad, every day and everywhere. Get mentored as you walk down the street. If you see something, consider it. Fight and bleed to understand a matter. That's mentorship.

In the military, we had a saying, "There is no such thing as a stupid question." No one should feel so self-conscious they avoid asking because it could be a life-or-death question. I would suggest you use the same mentality in the marketplace because we all have things we don't know. Don't be afraid to ask questions constantly as a small child does. If you do, people will respect the fact that you want to learn the nuts and bolts of everything. When you add that to the trust they already have for you, you're on your way to building a stable reputation among your coworkers.

A mature person will take hard advice and a mature person will leave someone's advice as well. Be open and be at choice.

One day the role will be yours to fill. When the time comes, it will be your turn to pass on wisdom and encouragement to other young bucks. You will know it's your time because people will randomly ask you questions. Yes, the student will become the teacher. This stewardship is a solemn responsibility for you to steward—a responsibility you could screw up if you let it go to your head. The more you care, the greater your influence will be.

Now you've graduated to the level of mentoring others. How do you know if you're a good one or not? There's a pretty good gauge out there to test yourself to see if you're being a good mentor. While thinking about the person and considering their situation, you should want them to pass you up in life. You should want them to make more money or sell more books than you. If something inside of you holds up and checks when considering this, you are not worthy to give advice.

YOU SHOULD WANT THEM TO OBTAIN MORE ACCOMPLISHMENTS THAN YOU. IF YOU CAN HONESTLY LOOK AT THEM AND SAY THAT IS TRUE, YOU ARE A GOOD MENTOR.

Biblical Perspective

There comes a time in a man's life when he crosses over from being a boy to becoming a man. Some would say it's when you leave your house, some would say it's when you turn eighteen, some would say it's when you get a job, some would say it's when you get married, some would say it's when you buy your first house or have your first kid. What do you think?

I think A BOY BECOMES A MAN WHEN HE GOES IN THE DIRECTION HE FEELS LED TO GO IN BY GOD AND NOT BY MAN. That shows the independence it takes to be an adult first, then a leader.

Yet there are so many examples of mentorship in the Bible. But it's more than that. I like to call it "generational catapulting." It's an interesting phenomenon we see if you consider the stories of the Bible with prayer and meditation. Check it out.

Joshua went where Moses couldn't.

Solomon gained more than David and built the temple when his father couldn't.

Elisha did double the miracles that Elijah did.

Jesus said that even greater things will be done by those who come after him.

The story of God has those who come up under another man of God to surpass them one day, doing more than they could have ever done. This takes a heart of those in higher leadership positions to be fine with the fact that their followers will go farther than them one day.

Thanks be to God that we also have examples of mentorship in the Bible when the wrong advice was taken. King Ahaziah was one of those who didn't understand this principle.

He too (King Ahaziah) followed the ways of the house of Ahab, for his mother encouraged him to act wickedly. He did evil in the eyes of the Lord, as the house of Ahab had done, for after his father's death they became his advisers, to his undoing. He also fol-

lowed their counsel when he went with Joram son of Ahab king of
Israel to wage war against Hazael king of Aram at Ramoth Gilead.
The Arameans wounded Joram; so he returned to Jezreel to recover
from the wounds they had inflicted on him at Ramoth in his battle
with Hazael king of Aram. (2 Chronicles 22:3–6)

Then Ahaziah son of Jehoram, king of Judah, went down to
Jezreel to see Joram son of Ahab because he had been wounded.

So yes, seek mentorship with the right heart, but also give the
last word to God.

Activation

Choosing a mentor might be hard. First, I'd like you to think back to a time when someone gave you a really good piece of advice, free of charge.

Do you have their face in your mind? Well, there you go, that's your mentor. Maybe you can create a regular cadence of asking them questions. Over time you may need to go in a separate direction, so don't make the mistake of tethering yourself to live the life someone else dictates to you. People change and you shouldn't feel obligated to sheep behind anyone, ever.

Also, make it a daily practice to ask yourself, "What would the me living twenty years from now tell me today?" Try it. Journal it and tuck it away for another day.

CHAPTER 21

Give Credit Where It Is Due, Quickly

If you want to build respect and trust with others, commend them without fail. It is vital for a leader to bring the best out in his or her people. This is a task a leader must adhere to, that to your followers, are most often caught, not taught. I guarantee you won't understand the value of this principle until you try it yourself a few times. A real leader recognizes the power their words carry. One way of using this power is to give credit where it is due.

Military Side

In the summer of 2006, my unit was deployed in one of the outskirt areas of Fallujah, Iraq. We were coming to the end of our deployment and the next platoon sent their advance team to meet us a week early to get a good handshake and a grasp of what we were doing. I paired up with their comms guy and showed them how we had done things for the past six months. During the transition, we had a disagreement.

The lower frequencies on the radio helped us reach to Marine assets farther away. The advance team didn't like that because if we were in a house talking to one another during a hit, lower frequencies had trouble punching through concrete walls. In Iraq, concrete is a popular construction material used and they were worried our personal radios wouldn't make clear contact inside of a building. So his team made the decision that they were going to use higher frequencies for their ops and gave us a few choice words for being so dumb not to. No big deal; special warfare guys are rough with one another and have to be for good reason.

We then went on a mission using their choice of frequencies on the radios and found out that we couldn't reach out and make solid comms with our marine evac helicopter unit to get picked up. Yup, that's bad. We had to reach out to our base, have them relay a message to their base that we were ready to get pulled out. A big deal. That night their guy came and found me immediately after we were back from the mission. He said, "I was wrong, and you were right. Good job."

As soon as he said that, a nice feeling of butterflies were set a flight in my soul! In all seriousness I thanked him for his honesty. Giving credit where credit is due.

Marketplace

Believe you me, in the SEAL teams, we don't just give positive credit for where credit is due; we also give negative credit. Truckloads of it. The saying goes, "A team guy who isn't bitchin is a dead team guy." We are always complaining about things in the world, in the country, in the military, in the Navy, and in our own teams. To be honest, that's the kind of personality that gets the ball rolling on things.

But a rough personality doesn't work in the civilian marketplace. Maybe in the upper echelon of corporations can you be rough with other executives, but not when you're dealing with lower-level professionals and trying to emerge as a leader that people want to follow. If you give too much negative feedback to people, they will begin to dislike your presence and you can forget about leading them.

So to make this simple for you, researchers have come up with a ratio for trust. That ratio is 30 to 1. For someone to trust you and listen to what you say, you have to not just give them negative feedback. So if you do give negative credit where negative credit is due, make sure you fill in the void area with thirty positive credits. Sorry for that, I know most people would think that's a little absurd and unimportant, but these are the things it takes for you to gain a following of people who trust you.

GIVING CREDIT TO PEOPLE IS LIKE ORGANIZING YOUR SOCK DRAWER. This goes here, that goes there. I'll put this behind that in my sock drawer is like organizing where you put credit where it belongs in your following. Some people are able to organize their homes well, but when it comes to organizing their team as a highly functioning unit, they don't have a clue. So help your workplace get organized, and if someone does a good job, give them a slap on the back.

Everyone is looking for someone to acknowledge them and tell them they've done a good job. There may be sometimes where people excel at what they're doing but never get the credit. That's your opportunity to take the place of a good leader and give credit where credit is due.

Biblical Perspective

Paul, the man who is credited with writing more books of the Bible than any other person in history, knew this principle very well. He honored people in every way he could. Look at how Paul exhorted people when he wrote to the church in Rome. All of Romans 16 was dedicated to giving credit to his followers. Don't worry, I have only highlighted the words where he gave credit to his followers.

I commend to you our sister Phoebe, a deacon of the church in Cenchreae. I ask you to receive her in the Lord in a way worthy of his people and to give her any help she may need from you, for *she has been the benefactor of many people*, including me. Greet Priscilla and Aquila, my co-workers in Christ Jesus. *They risked their lives for me*. Not only I but *all the churches of the Gentiles are grateful to them*. Greet also the church that meets at their house. Greet my dear friend Epenetus, *who was the first convert to Christ in the province of Asia*. Greet Mary, *who worked very hard for you*. Greet

Andronicus and Junia, *my fellow Jews who have been in prison with me. They are outstanding among the apostles, and they were in Christ before I was*. Greet Ampliatus, *my dear friend in the Lord*. Greet Urbanus, *our co-worker in Christ, and my dear friend* Stachys. Greet Apelles, *whose fidelity to Christ has stood the test*. Greet those who belong to the household of Aristobulus. Greet Herodion, *my fellow Jew*. Greet those in the household of Narcissus *who are in the Lord*. Greet Tryphena and Tryphosa, *those women who work hard in the Lord*. Greet my dear friend Persis, *another woman who has worked very hard in the Lord*. Greet Rufus, *chosen in the Lord*, and his mother, *who has been a mother to me, too.* Greet Asyncritus, Phlegon, Hermes, Patrobas, Hermas and the other brothers and sisters with them. Greet Philologus, Julia, Nereus and his sister, and Olympas and all the Lord's people who are with them. Greet one another with a holy kiss. All the churches of Christ send greetings. I urge you, brothers and sisters, to watch out for those who cause divisions and put obstacles in your way that are contrary to the teaching you have learned... The grace of our Lord Jesus be with you. Timothy, my co-worker, sends his greetings to you, as do Lucius, Jason and Sosipater, my fellow Jews. I, Tertius, who wrote down this letter, greet you in the Lord. Gaius, *whose hospitality I and the whole church here enjoy,* sends you his greetings.

Can you hear and feel the slobbering honor spilling all over the place here? Paul knows well how to give people credit, love and honor when it is due and he does so abundantly.

Activation

Today, keep an eye out for those who have done a superb job in their profession and let them know it, especially when it was difficult for them. Keep a special eye out for those who have done a good job going against the routine, political correctness, and the "group think" attitudes. They deserve double points from you.

CHAPTER 22

Fail Often and Early

The sweetest victory is the one that's most difficult. The one that requires you to reach down deep inside, to fight with everything you've got, to be willing to leave everything out there on the battlefield—without knowing, until that do-or-die moment, if your heroic effort will be enough. Society doesn't reward defeat, and you won't find many failures documented in history books.

Marketplace

The exceptions are those FAILURES THAT BECOME STEPPING-STONES TO LATER SUCCESS. Such is the case with Thomas Edison, whose most memorable invention was the light bulb, which purportedly took him one thousand tries before he developed a successful prototype. "How did it feel to fail one thousand times?" a reporter asked. "I didn't fail one thousand times," Edison responded. "The light bulb was an invention with one thousand steps."

Unlike Edison, many of us avoid the prospect of failure. In fact, we're so focused on not failing that we don't aim for success, settling instead for a life of mediocrity. When we do make missteps, we gloss over them, selectively editing out the miscalculations or mistakes in our life's resumé.

"Failure is not an option," NASA flight controller Jerry C. Bostick reportedly stated during the mission to bring the damaged Apollo 13 back to earth, and that phrase has been etched into our collective memory ever since. To many in our success-driven society, failure isn't just considered a non-option—it's deemed a deficiency.

Military Side

SEAL training revolves around failure and failing a BUD/S student constantly. Why? Because it builds a person to be untethered by the emotional fear of failure. This is an important quality and one you can develop.

Any teacher will explain to you a few things you should never do as a leader of a classroom. For example, you should never erase a chalkboard or whiteboard with a side-to-side motion because it makes your butt shake back and forth. I was trained this way because it's distracting. Not using red ink when grading papers and never telling someone they are wrong are other no-no's for teachers who desire to help people learn. It also becomes a hurdle to learning.

Yet in BUD/S, they bat you down with those same words all day, every day. We are told thing like, "you are a failure, how have you survived, everything you do is stupid." After six months of that, you end up chuckling to yourself any time someone tries to tell you this.

You see, this type of military training is used to get people to overcome the very important fear of failing, a very important quality for a soldier who wants to be the best. You should strive to have the same unemotional attachment in your life.

Now this doesn't mean you should be okay with failing. This is by no means an excuse for you to make decisions that lead to a business or personal failure. You should avoid it at all costs, by all means. You should never be satisfied with failing or coming up short. You should never allow yourself to carry out a plan that is unwise or lacking in planning.

For example, in everything we do in the Teams, we gather together in the end and debrief. This is a mandatory and very serious meeting where we go through each step of what we did and self-evaluate as a team. In our debriefs, we ask the hard questions. We call one another out if a mistake was made and we make operating procedure changes if necessary. Then we run it again.

Let me be clear though. Making certain mistakes are unacceptable at times. There are things that will get you kicked out of the teams. A habit of sweeping someone with your gun is one of those. A bad cocky attitude is another. For these mistakes, there is seldom remediation. Our program allows few mistakes and requires a "never give up" attitude.

Biblical Perspective

Being fine with failing often is a question of your surety pertaining to why you are doing whatever your thing is. If you take a position because of the return you'll get, that's great. What happens when the going gets tough and you don't get a return from your investment? Will you still do what you do?

Maybe God is making you a subject matter expert on the matter and failure is a part of teaching you that.

Jesus said, "My burden is light." Living for God is easy; it's abundant. At least it is when you have "oil in your lamp." So whether you fail or succeed, it's okay.

For Babe Ruth, he was fine with failure. He said that every strike brings him closer to his next home run. That kind of attitude made failing just fine with him.

The book of Ecclesiastes was written by King Solomon, and in it, he summarizes the whole point of life. As you read chapter 2, you can't help but see how it applies to being okay with failure.

You can't take it with you, so enjoy the process… I hated life, because the work that is done under the sun was grievous to me. All of it is meaningless, a chasing after the wind. I hated all the things I had toiled for under the sun, because I must leave them to the one who comes after me. And who knows whether that person will be wise or foolish? Yet they will have control over all the fruit of my toil into which I have poured my effort and skill under the sun. This too is meaningless. So my heart began to despair over all my toilsome labor under the sun. For a person may labor with wisdom, knowledge and skill, and then they must leave all they own to another who has not toiled for it. This too is meaningless and a great misfortune. What do people get for all the toil and anxious striving with which they labor under the sun? All their days their work is grief and pain; even at night their minds do not rest. This too is meaningless. A person can do nothing better than to eat and drink and find satisfaction in their own toil. This too, I see, is from the hand of God, for without him, who can eat or find enjoyment? To the person who pleases him, God gives wisdom, knowledge and happiness, but to the sinner he gives the task of gathering and storing up wealth to hand it over to the one who pleases God. This too is meaningless, a chasing after the wind. (Ecclesiastes 2:17–26 The Message)

As you can see, what is all the worry about failure? Why the stomachache? What's the deal with the fearing failure? Both good and bad stuff happens to all people, but A LEADER IS MADE BETTER BY THE MISTAKES.

Activation

Are you a failure? Have you failed? The answers to these two questions actually have no hold on the future. Why? Because your future has a whole new trajectory after you read this book.

You see, thinking that you're a failure isn't even a fact or fiction; it's simply an intangible thought. It's based on you comparing yourself to others. It's rooted in your wanting to save face in front of others and being okay with who you are and what you've done. Being okay with failing is first of all not caring what others think about you or what they say about you.

Your activation today is to tell that person in the mirror that you're not a failure and to stop comparing yourself to others.

CHAPTER 23

Have a Strong Stomach

As a leader, you need to exhibit a character trait that everybody learns to recognize. Young people, old people, your peers and even animals learn to recognize this. It's a primal leadership trait. You have to USE YOUR VOICE IN A WAY FOR YOUR WORDS TO BE TAKEN SERIOUSLY. It's a quality, that when you open your mouth, other people shut their mouth. When your words leave your mouth, they should pierce other people in the heart and not fall to the ground. This will take you from being a co-equal part of a functional team to being the leader of a functional team.

Military Side

One of the tiny slivers, among the vastness, of training in the military is learning something called verbal judo. It's the military's way of training a person to learn the power of their words. Verbal judo is basically shouting commands at people so they automatically listen with a primal urgency. Their mind doesn't process anything except carrying out the command. It's a fight-or-flight way of getting someone to take action. Similarly, prison guards and police officers use this technique of leadership and are trained to escalate the intensity in their voice very quickly upon seeing someone hesitate to follow orders.

We would use verbal judo to direct orders to people immediately after we blow down their door when assaulting a target. It's a voice of complete aggression and an offensive nature that allows zero rebellion.

Right now, you may be chuckling a little because you're thinking, "As much as I might like the image of blowing my boss's office door to smithereens, there's no way any kind of action like that is acceptable in the marketplace."

Well, you're right. Unless you're the chairman of a big corporation and you're yelling at your overpaid vice presidents, you're right. But your tone should be that of a person who is listened to.

It's up to you to learn how to do this in a professional manner. Yelling as a leader only means that your ability to lead is fragile. There is an ability I want you to be aware of that doesn't yell to get their words heard. It's a confident voice. ABUSING THIS LEADER-

SHIP CHARACTERISTIC CAN LEAD TO HARM IN OTHERS

AND A TIME BOMB IN YOUR CAREER GOALS.

Marketplace

There was a wise children's doctor who, while dealing with various kids, became very capable of dealing with all kinds of children's behaviors. One day he received a phone call from a mother who was concerned about a rash her eleven-year-old son had. She explained that whenever she asked her son to show it to her, he refused. She had taken him to other doctors, but he acted the same way. This new doctor was her last hope.

The doctor replied, "I'll see your son under one circumstance." Mother said, "Anything. What is it?" "When you come to our offices and I enter the room, you must do exactly as I tell you to do." "Really, that's it?"

"Yes."

Later that week, the mother brought her son to see the doctor. They went into the patient's observation room and waited. When the doctor came in, he said hello and abruptly stopped. He glanced over at the mother and said, "Can you please not stand there? Stand over there." He motioned to a spot a few feet away and the mother moved there.

He introduced himself to the young boy and then stopped again. He looked at the mother and said, "Please put your purse on the table." She did.

The doctor then said to the boy, "I hear you have a rash." The boy hesitated. The doctor looked again at his mother. "Please don't cross your arms." She immediately uncrossed her arms.

Turning his full attention to the boy, who willingly cooperated with the doctor, the boy described his rash. The difference between this doctor and the others is that he knew the power of his words. The boy's mother, and other doctors, didn't understand how to establish authority. The boy saw the others as weak while he saw this doctor as someone who should be listened to.

Now you have to take this principle and apply it to your cause. How do you interact with others? Are your words esteemed or do others take you for granted? If you honestly answer the question with "Others take me for granted," I have some hard advice for you.

First, start with changing your childlike mentality. Then move. Once you have grappled with this topic, it's time to relocate and start over. It's hard for people to allow a prince to become a king and that's what you're after. People have this way of holding you to the past. I would say first change your mentality, then merge into a new group of people with the same first impression this doctor used on the child with a rash.

Biblical Perspective

I wonder, if one were able to do so, what we would find to be the most stated subject matter of someone's "last words." As it goes with many families, these are the words that get reiterated many times over after they pass. We see this as King David passed his wisdom on. He chose to speak about strength.

When the time drew near for David to die, he gave a charge to Solomon his son. "I am about to go the way of all the earth," he said. "So be strong, act like a man. (1 Kings 2:1–2)

It takes the right mentality to be a successful leader. All that positive thinking prep talk you tell yourself in the morning is actually needed. Yes, you need to tell yourself you're a successful leader before you're successful. You need to tell yourself you are respected to be respected. You need to walk like a leader before you're a leader.

Activation

Today, walk like a leader. Talk like a leader. Choose your words carefully, then speak with clarity.

Be short. Be correct. Be inspiring. Be respected.

CHAPTER 24

Distinguish Yourself!

Empathy. If you possess it, many will fall in rank behind you.

If you care about people, they feel it. If you say, "How can I help you?" the other person sees someone who can be trusted and followed. People follow those who care more readily than for any other reason. Empathy allows you to keep your finger on the pulse of the people you're leading. It allows you to know if you're losing their faith, or if they are in lockstep with you.

Empathy extends influence in bottom-line and intangible measurements. EMPATHY IS THE GLUE THAT HOLDS TOGETHER THE GROWTH OF YOUR COMPANY OR GROUP. Without it, sales stagnate, morale collapses, teams compete with teams they should be collaborating with. You end up trying to muscle together things with your own strength and wit.

Here's a way of tangibly explaining the power of empathy. Let's say you own a company with more than fifty people. A leader who practices authentic empathy would have a lower attrition rate compared to a command-and-control leader. Instead of having 15 percent of employees find jobs elsewhere, only 3 percent will move elsewhere. So the end result is your hiring and training costs are lower.

Empathy will grow your company for you especially at the most critical times—when the only resource you really have to rely on is your people.

Military Side

The SEAL teams have a reverse leadership structure. It looks like an upside-down pyramid if you sketch it out on a piece of paper. Basically, the higher-ranking men work for the lower-ranking men helping them fulfill their duties. Funny enough, the Nordstrom company has uniquely mirrored this leadership structure.

Funny enough also is that everyone knows darn well the consequences of messing up do not flow in the same upside-down direction. Nope, not in the least. So if the men on the bottom of the pyramid aren't fulfilling their duties, you have to look at the leadership and ask them why.

This leadership style requires an officer to be understanding and empathetic to the men. It requires him to consider what exactly he is asking his men to do. This produces an atmosphere of confidence from the men because they trust the leadership to have their best intentions in mind.

Honestly, this is way better and more enjoyable than other military styles of getting work done. At the same time, it carries the assumption that each person is proactive, engaged, and willing that maybe the rest of the military units can't guarantee, so again, it's a unique method of leadership.

Marketplace

Interestingly enough, this distinguishing leadership character trait of empathy has also been found among primates. Frans De Waal is the author of *Alpha Male*. His book has become popular and respected in the past few decades for this research on chimpanzee tribes.

Recently he has explained that much of his research has led to a misunderstanding about what is actually the number one characteristic of the alpha male in a chimpanzee pack. He says it's empathy. This is actually the distinguishing aspect of an alpha male, not pomp.

The leader of the pack, alpha male, cares for the other male and female chimpanzees in the group. It was noticed that the male who dominated the other males made it a practice to regularly go around the females of the tribe to inspect for insects in their fur and rid them of parasites. Humans who desire top-level leadership should be profoundly serious about it too.

It's simple. IF YOU WALK AROUND PRIDEFULLY STOMPING OUT YOUR OPPONENTS, IT ACTUALLY GETS YOU THE OPPOSITE OF WHAT YOU WANt. It will get you the opposite of trust. Your followers won't hang on your words. They'll question your words and may think you have something else up your sleeve. This is an easily avoidable time bomb.

Biblical Perspective

One night as my wife and I were having a nice date, we noticed a pair of kids walking around from table to table talking with the patrons and handing out pieces of paper. They were taking a survey about the connection between violent video games and school shootings for a high school sociology class they were in. Little did they know when they arrived at our table what they got themselves into. As a deployed military vet during wartime, I had much to say about the psychology of violence. Needless to say, they didn't make it past our table too quickly.

So the conversation started. You've probably heard the term "adrenaline junkie." Well, as we spoke with the students, I added that the adrenaline you get from a video game is the same adrenaline you get in war, just on different levels.

The flagrant thing about everything virtual is that it's disconnecting people from others. That is what's concerning. It's all of social media, violent movies, and violent video games that have the same "disconnecting" effect. All 2D screens separate you from a 3D life of reality.

Hmm, disconnecting. Where have we seen that before? Well, that's a basic stipulation in the definition of someone who suffers as a sociopath. You read that right. *Sociopath* defined is "a person with a personality disorder manifesting itself in extreme antisocial attitudes and behavior and lack of conscience." Sociopaths do not have a sense of empathy or sympathy. This allows them to able to see and view other people in pain without being negatively affected. Does that sound like being disconnected to you? I'd say that all the electronic separations give people the ability to be desensitized to the general populous.

So I'm coining the phrase *micro sociopath*. Just like a sociopath is someone who is disconnected from feeling sympathy or empathy for someone else's suffering, a normal person would have sympathy for someone who is sick or got in a car accident. A sociopath doesn't have that ability. Most serial killers are sociopaths and they can do those indecent tasks because they are unable to feel emotion when other people suffer.

MANY PEOPLE IN OUR SOCIETY TODAY UNKNOW-INGLY GROW A MICRO SOCIOPATHIC ABILITY ONLINE. Think about it. Sometimes people purposefully slander or defame someone of a different political party or race on social media because they think it's okay to act and think that way. In fact, they desire for that person to suffer and be humiliated in a micro way. They actually desire for that person to suffer publicly and in this sense, they are comfortable with others suffering socially.

You see it every day on the news, and it's become somewhat of an accepted thing. People are constantly trying to publicly tear other people down so they are elevated and it's the opposite of what we call the gift of love.

What Paul says in 1 Corinthians 13 is that love cares for other people. It protects other people.

So the root of this chapter's lesson is really having the ability to carry someone else's heart. It's having empathy and sympathy for other people as you lead them in a good direction.

Activation

Do you have empathy? Don't answer that yourself. I want you to ask three of your closest friends if you are a person who possesses empathy. Journal those answers down and tuck them away for another day. When you're done with this book, bring them back out and read it again.

CHAPTER 25

Doubt and Confidence

At the time of this writing, the fastest supercomputer in the world has a maximum processing speed of 54.902 petaflops. A petaflop is a quadrillion (1,000 trillion) calculations per second. That's a huge number of calculations, and yet that doesn't even come close to the processing speed of the human brain.

Our miraculous brains are so fast, it is impossible to precisely calculate their speed, but a good guess is that the human brain operates at 1 exaflop, which is equivalent to a billion—billion calculations per second. Or thousands of times quicker than the fastest computer.

As quick as your brain is, it's also easily damaged and easily hurt by chemicals. Not many people realize that your body dumps only microscopic doses of chemicals into your bloodstream to make your brain feel an emotion. Melatonin, adrenaline, and others are only found in the tiniest amounts. That's how extremely sensitive your brain is.

The real difference between your brain and the K computer is that your brain can change itself. Your brain can actually change its operational ability. With simple discipline, you can stop or start a habit in a few days. How does this happen? In short, you have to believe that you can do something before you do it. This 'belief' in yourself is what changes your habits and abilities in your brain.

In this pursuit to become a better leader, some of us will need to change our brains and polish our leadership character and ability. In short, change our brain.

There is an old saying that goes like this: "Ninety percent of what I worried about was what I was afraid might happen. Truth is, those things I spent hours worrying over—never happened."

DOUBT SLOWS YOUR BRAIN DOWN. Doubt changes the chemical makeup of your brain. And doubt is the biggest killer of success. Doubt creates hesitation. Doubt stops you from beginning. Doubt is also a liar. It all starts in the mind.

The truth is you allow lies about yourself to circulate all day long in your vital supercomputer organ. All day long. I do too; everyone does. Let me ask you: how are you supposed to become a better you without changing how you think?

This is one of the most significant ways a future leader needs to become successful.

Before Jesus's ministry, the devil tried to attack this idea during his forty-day fast in the desert. If you read Matthew 4, one could paraphrase what the devil said: "Do a halfway job," "Follow my plan, not yours," and "Try a plan B." He tried to derail that greatest story in history by inserting a thought of self-doubt to Christ the Messiah. I would suggest he is doing the same thing to everyone else as well, and we listen. Self-doubt is a lie, instead you should spend your time thinking about how you will go full steam ahead with your cause, making the world a better place.

Marketplace

We all know very well the motorcycle brand Harley-Davidson. What you may not know is how it emerged from the hundreds of other motorcycle brands out there.

A twenty-one-year-young William Harley drafted a gasoline engine that could fit into a bicycle frame. He then went on to recruit the three Davidson brothers to join him in his motorcycle takeover of a new market of transportation.

They had no plan B; the four bike lovers hunkered down in their garage to make the best bike. They didn't do anything other than think and work about ways to push the new motorcycle brand. Harley-Davidson went big because they publicized their company and put it on the stock market, allowing investors to get behind the brand. This won them loyalty and funds to build a bigger factory. They also recruited dealers to sell their bikes in the states and world-wide overseas.

All the other motorcycle makers stayed small and used their own money to grow (Did you see the doubt?). Because he didn't have doubt in himself, Harley was even able to score the beginning of the name on the logo. Harley-Davidson represents four people: him and the three Davidson brothers. But he got the first half of the name split because he was a leader who didn't doubt himself. Even nowadays, we abbreviate the brand with just saying "Harley." This is what it looks like when someone goes all in.

Military Side

As part of the Naval Special Warfare units, I know what it's like to apply myself to become something bigger. SEAL training does change you. Training breaks you down physically and mentally but builds a warrior in the mind. Some people debate that SEAL training doesn't build a mindset in people, but it finds the people who hold the right mindset already. I believe that BUDs just proves to you that you were right about yourself and your abilities. Either way, what makes a man worthy of the SEAL teams is in the mind.

Right before I exited the Navy, a group of researchers were compiling information on Navy SEALs. They were trying to find out what similar characteristics people had to make it into the teams. They hoped to use that information to recruit more effectively that demographic, but they came up unsuccessful and almost empty-handed, except for three pieces of information. They found a correlation between age, life experience, and nationality.

One significant piece of information they found pertained to what nationality made it through at the highest ratio. Can you guess what race of people was most successful? Mexicans, or like my Mexican buddies in the teams would say, Mexi-"CAN." For some reason, Mexicans graduate seal training at a 65 percent rate.

Another distinguishing aspect they found is that a trainee had to have gone through tough life experiences. A previous arduous life before training is the common denominator for someone who wanted to make it through to become something better than they were. ONE OF THE BIGGEST FAULTS OF YOUNG PEO-

PLE IS THAT THEY DON'T USE THEIR PAINFUL YEARS. HUMBLING TIMES ARE THE BEST THINGS THAT HAPPEN TO PEOPLE. It makes you who you are, so don't waste your pain!

Other findings of people who have made it through training involved age. Students eighteen to twenty-two years old had a 5 percent chance of success and students twenty-two to twenty-eight years old had about 25 percent chance of making it through. I honestly think the age factor reflects maturity and a larger amount of pain experienced in life. The more pain you've lived through, the more success you'll have.

An interesting aspect of SEAL training is that it is distinguished from other military schools by a unique focus—a focus uncommon to every single other elite program in the world. BUD/S training revolves around *constantly* failing a student. All day long, every day the student works incredibly hard, yet is told he is a failure even when he's not. If he does complete something amazing, he's a failure. No other program in the military does that. Its purpose is to find those who can endure the chaos of the battlefield while continuing to fight.

The point is to build a soldier with confidence in himself. Then to take those individuals and knit them together as a team. Teams are powerful, but when team members are instilled with a belief in their ability, watch out. There's a reason they called the SEALs to get Bin Laden. Confidence.

Biblical Perspective

Riddle me this. Why is it that someone who is poor and wins the lottery and gets rich almost always loses it all and is poor again? Then you have a billionaire who loses everything in a bad economy, yet again one day is a billionaire once more? I'd say it's this principle of being confident to make the right decisions without doubting themselves, has a lot to do with putting your money to work for you. IF YOU DOUBT YOURSELF, YOU WON'T INVEST IN YOURSELF, thus taking your earnings and spending it on things that don't make you more money.

The stingy are eager to get rich and are unaware that poverty awaits them. (Proverbs 28:22)

This principle King Solomon speaks of is one that pierces doubting yourself. So take what you believe to be true and have the confidence.

Activation

Take a moment to think to isolate yourself from all distractions. Turn off your devices. Ask yourself what gives you the biggest reasons to pause before diving into your investing of yourself. What creates doubt?

Take those items and erase them for your identity. I guarantee you, others can see them, especially other investors.

CHAPTER 26

Build Culture

When you think about business, you may immediately think about a business plan. How much money would be needed? Who are the competitors in the market? Then how much energy and time you're willing to give to it?

Let me ask you, do you ever think about creating a positive culture? How to get a smile on people's faces?

You might think, that doesn't have anything to do with business. In reality, it's the very glue that holds the fabric of our marketplace together in every way. WHETHER YOU KNOW IT OR NOT, YOU ARE SELLING HAPPINESS, A SMILE, OR AN ENDORPHIN RELEASE TO OTHERS. PERIOD. Your followers listen to you for that reason. Strategy and forward momentum are one thing, culture is the other.

This is a relatively new principle in our business world; it hasn't always been that way. A hundred years ago, Henry Ford could throw you on the streets for not keeping up with the assembly line; it didn't matter if you were hurt or disabled while on the job. Even though Mr. Ford is credited with many positive attributes, truth is, he cultivated a very fear-filled culture within the workplace. Why? Because times were different and he could.

Let's contrast with twenty years ago, owners and bosses could talk how they wished because the internet wasn't around to expose them yet. The "he said, she said" days are over, and no doubt, so are the "guilty until proven innocent" idea as well. Let me ask you, if you don't convey a good culture and people feel a hint of any ism, do you think they would blast out on the World Wide Web that you actually are that ism?

Yet now, everyone knows everything. The grapevine has grown some legs, and you need to implement a good culture. With the popularity of social media, your customers can control your reputation.

This doesn't imply that you should create a good culture so you don't get caught doing bad things. You should create a good culture because it's leading others in a "good direction."

Marketplace

A good culture and friendly atmosphere are very important. While this may be taught in MBA courses, it's too often forgotten in the competitive marketplace. Learning this lesson sometimes has to come from the school of hard knocks. Experience is required.

In late 2018, articles started coming out about how Facebook's employee culture was beginning to sour. People were jumping ship for this one reason. My analysis, simplified, was that Mr. Zuckerberg once had a new and exciting idea, but that idea outgrew the honeymoon. The initial excitement was overwhelmed by the amount of work, and Mark had to create something—a positive culture in the workplace.

Without the excitement, what should Mark do? Can he do anything? Throw more company parties? Give out bonuses?

Military Side

Some people might ask what is the culture in the SEAL teams. Well, we are a very motivated group. You're talking about a group of men, all of whom are at the peak of their physical ability of their life, all of whom accepted the toughest challenge on earth, and all of whom made it and are now on the same team. The culture was a "We are the best. If not us, no one is going."

Now each SEAL team is made up of a number of platoons. This number is more than 1 but less than 734. Each platoon consists of sixteen men, each has a different job, but all men know how to do one another's duties. These platoons are led by one enlisted man and one officer. The interesting thing you can see happening with each platoon is how the men usually follow the personality of their leadership. Each lieutenant and chief brings a certain flavor to the unit. Whether it's a "by the book" attitude or a "full-bore balls to the wall breakneck speed" attitude, the identity and culture are carved out by the platoon leaders. It was actually pretty easy to distinguish a platoon by the way they acted.

These attitudes created reputations for each platoon during our training cycles as reports were given from the training staff to the team CO, EO, and CMC—that is, commanding officer, executive officer, and command master chief. The team leadership would use this identity and culture within the platoons to decide which area the team would deploy to.

You see, each region of the world needed different things. Let me see if I can explain this any better. The calculus function of war required certain inputs for certain outcomes. This calculus function is different from region to region.

The platoon culture is also a driver of determining where it would deploy to. Each platoon with it's individual culture was considered for regional calculus. The same is true when your company or group is considered for hire.

Now that might be a little different than establishing a good workplace culture, but can you see the cause and effect? You as a leader must make a purposeful plan and build your group around a solid cultural plan. Without being able to establish a good culture, you're unable to be promoted as a leader.

Have you ever heard of someone who spent a month or more in the South and came back talking like a Southern bell? What happened? They were affected by the culture. It rubbed off on them.

It was said about President Obama that the culture of the White House staff was a very unpatriotic culture. On the other hand, it has been said that President Trump had created a very volatile culture.

I would say both presidents didn't intend or try to create this culture but that it just happened. Their energy and presence affected the people around them.

AS A LEADER, YOU'VE GOT TO BE AWARE AND INTENTIONAL ABOUT WHAT CULTURE YOU CREATE. IT

DOESN'T HAVE TO BE "THIS" OR "THAT." YOU JUST HAVE TO KNOW THAT YOU ARE MAKING YOUR BED AND YOU HAVE TO SLEEP ON IT.

Do you want to have a "work hard" culture? Be careful you don't also build a burnout reputation as well.

Do you want to have a "fun" culture? Be careful, your employees do not take their job for granted.

Do you want to build a "high energy," "highly professional" culture? Good for you. Good luck.

Biblical Perspective

But if serving the Lord seems undesirable to you, then choose for yourselves this day whom you will serve, whether the gods your ancestors served beyond the Euphrates, or the gods of the Amorites, in whose land you are living. But as for me and my household, we will serve the Lord. (Joshua 24:15)

Can you hear the heart-pumping-culture building Joshua was making? He wanted it known that the culture of his family was going to be a culture that honored God. It gets in your bones.

King David set the culture of his kingdom from the front. He led the people by example, not with word but with action. He set the culture of his kingdom to be one that wasn't ashamed before man to follow the Lord.

And David danced before the Lord with all his might; and David was girded with a linen ephod. So David and all the house of Israel brought up the ark of the Lord with shouting, and with the sound of the trumpet. And as the ark of the Lord came into the city of David, Michal Saul's daughter looked through a window, and saw king David leaping and dancing before the Lord; and she despised him in her heart. (2 Samuel 6:14–16)

You know, isn't it funny how the leaders of the nation of Israel had importance placed on them from the Lord to follow him? It is true that as goes the king, so goes the people. It was a lesson in both spiritual warfare and leadership for setting the right culture among your people.

This is spiritual warfare because leaders are the gateways that give entitlements to principalities of the air. These principalities either have access or are denied access to regions because of the sin or righteousness of a leader. That's you.

But when the judge died, the people returned to ways even more corrupt than those of their ancestors, following other gods and serving and worshiping them. They refused to give up their evil practices and stubborn ways. (Judges 2:19)

Even after this, Jeroboam did not change his evil ways, but once more appointed priests for the high places from all sorts of people. (1 Kings 13:33)

Moreover, the word of the Lord came through the prophet Jehu son of Hanani to Baasha and his house, because of all the evil he had done in the eyes of the Lord, arousing his anger by the things he did, becoming like the house of Jeroboam—and also because he destroyed it. (1 Kings 16:7)

But the people did not listen. Manasseh led them astray, so that they did more evil than the nations the Lord had destroyed before the Israelites. "Manasseh king of Judah has committed these detestable sins. He has done more evil than the Amorites who preceded him and has led Judah into sin with his idols... Moreover, Manasseh also shed so much innocent blood that he filled Jerusalem from end to end—besides the sin that he had caused Judah to commit, so that they did evil in the eyes of the Lord." (2 Kings 21:9–11, 16)

APPROACHING THE RESPONSIBILITY OF SETTING THE CULTURE SHOULD STRIKE THE FEAR OF THE LORD IN ANYONE WHO ASPIRES TO BE A LEADER. It's a grave responsibility because you justify or abolish so much without uttering a single word.

Activation

If your people aren't smiling, why? Do you know why? Here is a list of things that might be chipping away at your culture and the retention of your people.

Has the culture fragmented? Do they favor some over others? That'll take a smile away. You got to crush the cliques! Make everyone feel equal!

Are they appreciated?

Do they feel listened to, valued? Sometimes it's as easy as listening to what people have to say.

Are you a jerk? Maybe not with your words but with your body language you might be.

Do you host seasonal gatherings for social improvement?

Is your promotional system unfair?

Hopefully, you allow yourself an unbiased self-assessment. The litmus test for your culture is your employees' facial expressions. If people aren't happy and motivated, their eyes will tell.

CHAPTER 27

Take Your Boss's Job Away

One of the principles we live by in the SEAL teams is "take your boss's job away from him." This means that you are so proactive and resourceful in completing training or mission-essential tasks that the person over you has to do nothing more than check in to make sure it's done.

Marketplace

I was talking with the vice president of Sears a while back and he was explaining to me about the relationship he had with his boss, the president. When he took the executive position, his boss explained that he had an open-door policy and that anyone was welcome to approach him at any time. Now that's a great policy to have and makes for great morale at the company. He then explained that if he was approached too often to help figure some issues out, that was fine. "I'm here to help, but then why am I paying you if I'm always figuring things out for you?" It made him feel expendable and set the tone for a reality of what drives your paycheck.

As a rising leader, we should lean into every detail and get things going in a proactive way. Don't wait to be asked or told what to do. Have it already done. Be ahead of the task.

Military Side

There is a tremendous amount of work that goes into planning a SEAL mission. We must know everything about everything before we go. We all must know one another's job. To plan a mission, it takes sixteen guys planning a mission in three days or so. Two days of planning is breakneck speed and most likely allows for less-than enough sleep.

When we do all our work and those appointed over us don't have to assist us, they are able to focus on more important things. At times we would even ask if we could take their gun and gear to prep before going on a mission or to clean it after a mission.

Imagine for a moment what this looks like in the workplace. What things does your boss stress about and how can you help them focus more on the things above your level in the company? Here are a few things that will stick out to your boss.

Be proactive and ask them what they need. Just the fact that you're asking to take some of the load off of their plate screams that you're ready for a promotion. Yet I would suggest it's better if you figure this out without asking.

Don't bring your drama to work. Telling your boss about the drama in your life, whether at work or at home, makes their job harder. They already carry the mantle of leading your team, so make it easier for them and help carry their yoke. Replace your drama with a smile. Take notes so your boss doesn't have to repeat their words to you. It also shows them you're engaged.

If you are able to do these things, you've just taken a step to becoming a leader yourself.

This is because true leadership is serving, and if you learn to serve, you'll excel faster than the selfish people around you even if you're younger. To be a great leader, you must first learn to be a good follower. It requires contentment with your current position before you get the next.

Trust me when I say that if you're not content with your current position or job, it's a barrier to putting in the extra work. IF

YOU DON'T PUT IN THE EXTRA WORK TO SERVE, YOU

WON'T BE CONTENT WITH THE NEXT POSITION. What

needs to change isn't what's outside of you; it's what's inside of you.

This makes serving others above and below you simple and easy.

Biblical Perspective

You are the hands and feet of Christ.

Have you ever seen someone healed? If you have, have you

ever seen them healed without someone praying for them? Doubt it.

Although God cannot be put in a box, I bet the number is low.

Some people think the gift of healing is only for a few. I

BELIEVE IT IS FOR ALL. I LIKE TO CALL IT AN ANSWER

TO A BOLD PRAYER, NOT THE GIFT OF HEALING. It was

a prayer that was answered. You see, 100 percent of all prayers that

are not prayed go unanswered.

So Christ's way of dictating the manifested signs of the Holy

Spirit to his followers is to have them do his job. No?

Activation

Take some time today to think about ways to make your boss's jobs easier for them and limit the time you spend thinking about yourself, without brownnosing! Journal it. If you can do this, your promotion is almost guaranteed.

CHAPTER 28

As a Leader, You Are Accountable

Many high-level leaders believe the rules don't always apply to them. For example, if they make a mistake, or don't exercise professional etiquette, they know that they're probably not going to be called out for it.

For example, Mark Zuckerberg doesn't always choose to wear a suit and tie to his board meetings, but instead, he wears a sweatshirt. Why? Because he can. He's the boss. Today I want to show you that this is a slippery slope.

The problem here isn't unpolished shoes; the problem is a mentality. Over time those under you will lose faith. Your leadership will deteriorate if you don't allow yourself to be held accountable while at the top of your group. It will begin to crumble. Your employees won't value the business because of a leader who's not accountable. They'll say, "If he/she doesn't care, then neither should I."

This leader doesn't feel it's necessary to do the little things in themselves and the employees will only fall in line with the same kind of thinking.

Let me ask you, why should they value the business if you don't appear to? If you don't show pride then they won't either and their willingness to come to work boils down to money to sustain their lifestyle. Instead of working for you to change the world or further a good cause, they are only there because they need a paycheck. That's like paying people to be your friends. It is the end result of a leader who chooses not to be held accountable.

As a leader, you need to get over yourself, fight laziness, show pride in your appearance, and little details. It will trickle down into the value of your organization in a positive way.

Military Side

In the army's leadership manual, it outlines the six characteristics of leadership.

The characteristics are broken down into three attributes and three competencies. The military gives "presence" one-sixth of the weight of being a leader.

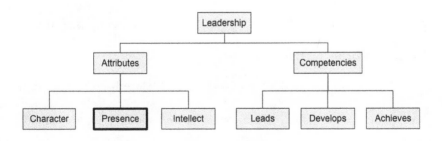

That's huge. The Army defines 'presence' as having a military bearing (dressing the part), professional bearing (same thing), fitness, confidence, and resilience.

You may ask, what does presence have to do with being accountable? Well, when you present yourself crisp, professional and clean, it says, "I value myself and I value this team and I value this cause." Having a presence makes people turn their heads and notice. It makes you someone others want to be like. Do you value yourself enough to forge a leader's presence? Make yourself accountable.

Marketplace

The 1992 Olympic basketball team the USA fashioned is regarded as the best sports team ever assembled in the history of sports. They were labeled the dream team. Michael Jordan, Scottie Pippen, Magic Johnson, Charles Barkley, Larry Bird, Patrick Ewing, David Robinson, John Stockton, Karl Malone, Clyde Drexler, Chris Mullin were selected. All were Hall of Famers and all were at the peak of their careers. When they played together, people said it was like poetry being written.

They were coached by the wise Chuck Daly, who was a man of few words. He didn't say much, but when he spoke, people listened.

He was perfect for the job as he knew how to coach men of such caliber. It wasn't his knowledge of the game that made him succeed; it was his knowledge of leading players. Each player alone could have led the team to a win. This team had eleven of them. How do you take eleven kings and make them work together?

The first thing he made sure the players knew was that they were accountable. His first lecture was to be the most profound. When the first team meeting came, everyone wondered what he was going to say. This is what he did:

He asked each person to be on time to the team meetings. That's it.

The players thought it would have been more prolific, specific, or strategic. As what might be a surprise to you, Chuck Daly knew what attitudes might make people think they weren't accountable. So he got each king of their own court to respect one another and show up on time.

Can you imagine what might happen if Charles Barkley would have pumped up his ego and decided a few times that he would sleep in? What would the other players think? I bet they would have said the same thing: "I'm not showing up on time. I'd be the only one. If they are late, then I'll be late." Can you see the value diminish?

Showing up on time gives respect for the group and the value they had for one another. How much more should you value your team and be accountable to your appearance and value your employee's time.

No student can surpass their teacher. As such, no business can be more valuable than its leader. Your employees won't surpass you in your professionalism; you must lead them there.

Allow me to go deeper. If this is a challenge for you, why? I want you to ask yourself a question. Is it possible you might struggle with a low self-value? Are you not worth buying yourself nice clothes? Do you feel less than worthy of presenting yourself professionally? If you answer with hesitation, you have some deep-rooted problems that I would guess stem from other things. If you want to be real to yourself and be successful, it's time to take one step back so you can take two steps forward. Talk with a professional and ask them to help you reevaluate your self-perception as one of value.

Hypothetically, what happens when a person with low self-value has a bad day one day and a skeleton from the past comes out of the closest? What do you do then? What happens if you get fired or have tremendous loss? What then? Just a heads-up: a person with low self-value must address the root of the issue. Otherwise, it's a time bomb waiting for you in the future.

This topic leads to a great conversation with yourself. It's a deep thought that requires a deeper conversation within yourself.

Biblical Perspective

As a leader, you are held to a higher level of responsibility. You cannot expect the people that follow you to exude a better professionalism than you do. To do so is unrealistic and unbiblical.

Not many of you should become teachers, my fellow believers, because you know that we who teach will be judged more strictly. (James 3:1)

Although James is speaking of being judged in your heavenly life, it relates to this present life as well.

Just the same, Jesus also washed the feet of each and every one of his twelve disciples (even Judas), showing that people shouldn't be above anyone else. This principle didn't make sense to Peter and he tried to resist his "teacher" from washing his feet, but it was necessary. Jesus was trying to show them this very principle.

You see, if you account yourself to be above professionalism among your people, that's pride. And we all know what comes after pride... A fall. If it comes later that day, year, or decade, a fall will happen.

Activation

Go the extra mile. Get up a little earlier to get ahead of the day. Prep your clothes the night before. Arrive early and be prepared. Sit with a leader's posture and set the tone of having pride in your entity (good pride). This, too, will trickle down and help you become a good leader.

C H A P T E R   2 9

How Dare You!

It is my strong belief that baseball isn't really a sport. I mean, seriously, do we think that standing around for 98 percent of the game takes stamina, strength, or talent?

If I could go back in time to meet the person who thought up the sport, I would have liked to see how weak of a person he was to try and figure out a sport so he could feel valued as a human. Maybe he was slow, unathletic, and couldn't keep up playing a real man's sport, like football.

Before you react, think about what I just did there. If I offended you or got under your skin, guess what? I did it on purpose. I manipulated you to control what you did with your mind. I made your mind get judgmental and maybe upset with only a few simple words.

Being offended, getting reactive, gives your power away. Why give others control of what you do? Why would you allow someone else to determine if you are happy or sad? Motivated or depressed? Leaders don't respond according to what others do; they respond out of who they are on the inside.

Marketplace

In drug rehab therapy, they call a negative emotional response a trigger. Triggers are things that irritate you, and if you've ever been through a rehab program, you've probably learned to identify them. You would then learn to delete them by role-playing or imagining you are in the situation and then going through the proper emotional reaction you should have in that situation. Otherwise, in a moment of frustration or irritation, you might go back to your comfort drug or make other bad decisions.

A professional leader does the same in the workplace. LEADERS KNOW THERE IS NO END TO THE NUMBER OF FIRES ONE HAS TO PUT OUT IN A DAY. The problem comes when it wears on you and becomes a trigger. Maybe you bring it home to affect your family life, your energy, and your professional character and reputation.

There is a way to identify people who live with wounds from offenses. This may help you hire certain people or not. They go from job to job, friendship to friendship, and possibly marriage to marriage. The effects of being offended aren't seen instantly, but over a few decades, the diagnosis is quite simple and takes the shape of this pattern. The beginning of a certain relationship is great as they haven't had a history of offenses up to that point. There are hellos and goodbyes every day. Work projects are easily communicated, and there's a good amount of productivity.

Once something happens, it's hard for the offended party to view other coworkers or friends as they did before the offense, and a death spiral starts. It can look like this:

First, the person conceals that they were offended. E-mail responses are delayed, and text responses are one-worded. Work projects become difficult, arduous, and slow because of this poison in the pond. As soon as a failure pops up, the blame pops on the scene like a freshly popped piece of popcorn.

Whenever I meet a person who is easily offended, I have to hold myself back when what I'd really like to do is one of the most loving and caring things possible. I'd like to take their face off and punt it twenty years into the future and show them what becomes of acting this way. I would show them their future self…an unhappy, unfulfilled person with, maybe, broken relationships and failed business ventures.

In the emotional moment with all the blame and emotions, someone feels justified. It takes integrity and commitment and wisdom, to take a deep breath, and move beyond reaction and think about what you would like to make happen.

Military Side

During SEAL training, the instructor staff has a very keen eye for those who can't get along and play nice with the others. If during the many evolutions students do, they are found out, their name goes into the "book of woes." If your name goes into the "book of woes," you don't get much help from anyone when you need it. It is also a signal to position you right next to others who get mad and offended, just like you do. Kiss your Team guy dreams away when that happens; the spotlight is already on you and your attitude. Placing two BUDs students with attitude next to each other gets them to push each other more and makes the instructor staff able to get them to quit quicker. We don't want them, we can't afford that attitude behind a gun under pressure.

What are some of your triggers? Do you get offended? Do certain things make you act in an unprofessional way? Politics, religion, office situations? Do those situations crawl in your head and take time away from you being productive or nice? Do you lose control over your facial expressions and body language? Why? It's unproductive and it will never get you a good reputation. I would say that if you want to be a great person, then be a great person because you choose to be, not because your surrounding situations make you great.

IF YOU'RE GOING TO SET VALUES AND STANDARDS FOR YOURSELF, DON'T LET OTHER PEOPLE ROB YOU OF THOSE VALUES AND MANIPULATE WHAT YOUR MIND OR BODY DOES AND WHAT YOUR MOUTH SPEAKS. Don't let others affect your posture and slouch over or take time away from your job in your head.

Biblical Perspective

Not being offended is hard and I believe comes with seasoned practice of forgiving people. You see, my road to not being offended started only because Christ said to forgive, not because I wanted to. As I pursued God, there were items of unforgiveness in my heart and mind. So I went through each of those things one by one and forgave them one by one. Each time it happened, there was a sweet aroma and it was like a weight had been taken off.

But then, just as the apostle Paul predicted, more offenses came. I would get offended and then later I would have to circle back during my devotional time with the Lord and forgive that person for that item. After a while of forgiving people for various things, even little things, it occurred to me that I was wasting my time by being offended in the first place.

Forgiveness is a powerful tool, but not taking offense is even more powerful. It allows you to think and operate free from external manipulation. It is liberating. It is leadership in a good direction if you teach others to do the same. And just like all these other principles, it is extremely lucrative business to practice.

It seems that when we obey God's Word, it's not only pleasing to him, but it benefits us at the same time.

Bearing with one another and, if one has a complaint against another, forgiving each other; as the Lord has forgiven you, so you also must forgive. (Colossians 3:13)

Then Peter came up and said to him, "Lord, how often will my brother sin against me, and I forgive him? As many as seven times?" Jesus said to him, "I do not say to you seven times, but seventy times seven. "Therefore the kingdom of heaven may be compared to a king who wished to settle accounts with his servants. When he began to settle, one was brought to him who owed him ten thousand talents. And since he could not pay, his master ordered him to be sold, with his wife and children and all that he had, and payment to be made. (Matthew 18:21–35)

And whenever you stand praying, forgive, if you have anything against anyone, so that your Father also who is in heaven may forgive you your trespasses. (Mark 11:25)

Activation

Take some time and list five of your triggers. Then list how you will respond, with awareness now, when those triggers occur.

This is your plan. Make sure you follow it.

CHAPTER 30

Timing Can Be Everything, Defibrillate Your Team

'Timing can be everything' is a chapter equipping you with a tool, not a principle. What you get today is something to put in your toolbox for another day. Tuck it away and be aware of your abilities once established as a leader.

When I finished my enlistment in the military, I moved to the northern part of the country and needed a place to stay for a little while I did some job hunting. A distant family relative and nice old man opened his house to my wife and me. During the three months we stayed there, I would sit at the dinner table with him for prolonged hours talking about life.

Marketplace

He is an avid fisherman, retired math teacher, high school chess coach, and one heck of a jokester. He would tell me of pranks that he pulled when he was younger. Some were so funny it would make milk come out of a person's nose (okay, mine).

He let me in on a life secret. While he coached the school chess team, some of his players began to be really successful. One year, three players were invited to the state chess championship tournament. It was about two-and-a-half-hour drive to get there. This was before phones and GPS, and because it was so far away, he offered to drive the three students he had who made the cut.

On the way he pretended that he had taken a wrong turn and was lost. He was not, but he played it out verbally saying that he "kind of knew where he was" and he "might know where he was going." He told the kids that if they didn't make it to the chess tournament that he was sorry and maybe next year they could have another shot at it. Imagine the thoughts going through those players' heads. All the hard work these kids had put into chess that year would have all been for nothing. They were scared and nervous. Little did they know that this wise man was helping their body produce adrenaline. Miraculously, or so they thought, they got to the chess tournament on time, even a little early. Those kids were relieved, filled with adrenaline that enabled them to focus on their chess games like never before. They also swept the state competition. I'd say the fear of missing the tournament caused them to fear which enabled them to focus better than the other players who sweated and stressed all day thinking about playing. As leaders, we focus on keeping our people happy, but sometimes we have to be open to the possibility of helping them in ways not so obvious. Timing is, of course, everything.

Right now, you might be saying this isn't a very nice or ethical leadership tool; it sounds more like a nasty prank you'd pull on someone, potentially disqualifying you as a leader. I would say it's a vital one if you ever need to get your team focused for your cause. It's also a way for you to see who cares and who doesn't care about your cause based on the reaction to the situation.

Chuck Daly who coached the 1992 Olympic basketball dream team used this tool as well. The first time he brought his team in to play a scrimmage practice, he also gathered a bunch of college basketball players to play these eleven fantastic men. During the scrimmage, he let these Hall of Famers play freely and figure out for themselves their own roles on the court. They were all leaders of their respective teams and now they had to figure out how they could come together.

During the game, he kept rotating the players and switching the matchups while the college kids were allowed to keep playing with the same guys. The dream team ended up losing their first basketball scrimmage to a bunch of kids to their own bewilderment. But it was on purpose and Chuck Daly knew that he had to get the attention of his men and scare them into humility and listening to him.

He rotated his players on purpose and didn't play Michael Jordan as much as the other players because he purposefully wanted them to lose to these collegiate athletes. It made them focus the whole rest of the year because Chuck was able to remind them with a commonly used phrase: "You could lose." He didn't even tell the other assistant coaches what he was up to because this was an art of a well-trained leader that the assistants wouldn't have understood.

Military Side

Just like the chess coach and Chuck Daly, understand that the common denominator in these situations is the chemical of adrenaline and the effect it has on the human body. The brain gets an injection of this chemical and your heartbeat quickens. Blood races to the muscles and prepares them for strenuous work. This is the same fight-or-flight chemical soldiers get on the battlefield.

I'm sure you have heard stories of grandmothers lifting cars off of people's bodies after a car accident. That's adrenaline. It comes when you get scared and not very many other times. In the military, you face situations on the battlefield that fill your body with the same chemical. Bullets bouncing off the pavement ahead of you or cracking over your head produce this adrenaline. Some operators are called "adrenaline junkies" because battle brings a bit of a high along with it.

Consider for yourself, as a leader, how at times you're able to get your team's attention and bring the adrenaline of the battlefield into your office...in a good way. HOW CAN YOU GET BATTLEFIELD FOCUS AND GRIT INTO THE BONES OF YOUR FOLLOWERS? That's a question for you to answer. A tool every good leader should know is there.

Biblical Perspective

If you didn't know, God is so good! Now you know. He does some amazing things among us. When my daughter was five years old, she had an amazing dream about Jesus's resurrection over Easter weekend. In it, she recounted three things that weren't written in the Scriptures.

One of those things was that when Jesus appeared to his disciples behind closed doors, they cheered. Then they asked if Jesus would then take over the country militarily. According to her dream, the disciples were still thinking the Messiah was a military savior, not a heavenly Deliverer. A physical takeover instead of the spiritual one God had in mind.

You can see in prior scriptures that the disciples wanted to overthrow the Roman government system. I can see how that would have also been derived from examining the Old Testament prophets who told about the Messiah being a Deliverer as well.

Then Jesus died and they were all confused. They thought he was the Messiah and now he died. They were even gathered together in a room talking and sharing their thoughts when he appeared.

His instructions were to not do anything before they had the power of the Holy Spirit from on high.

At this particular time, the eleven disciples were fully focused and fully ready to play as a team. They had a sudden scare and adrenaline was pumping. They were confused and scared because they were thinking in terms of human standards. This made them stay and focus in ways they wouldn't have done before.

Their direction from Jesus was to "stay and wait for the power." Like all other growth in the Lord, it takes real hunger for God. Real praying and fasting with humility. I'd say this was achieved. When Pentecost came and they all spoke in tongues, they were ready for their launch.

Time was leveraged. Take that and do the same to lead others in a good direction.

Activation

Only at certain times in your career should you put your group in situations like this. If you try to control the situation and scare your people so that they perform better, just know that at the same time you could also lose their trust. JUST LIKE A BABY SNAKE HAS THE MOST POTENT BITE BECAUSE IT RELEASES ALL OF ITS VENOM, SO DOES A YOUNG LEADER USE ALL OF THEIR TOOLS WITHOUT WISDOM. If you indeed want to be a good leader, save this leadership tool for the right situation.

CHAPTER 31

Building Trust

As small companies get larger, they outgrow the ability to have leaders and managers provide personal direction. With more employees, corporations and groups, replace human guidance with policies and procedures. This is a necessary step, but with the limited interaction with the leaders, it can also restrict innovation, team morale, and just basic communication.

There is an acronym we used in the SEAL teams: KISS. Keep It Simple Stupid. This is important to remember from the smallest details concerning yourself to the big components of an operation with your platoon. While planning missions, we have to know everything about everything, and then more. We have to construct an ironclad plan for everything that might go wrong (Murphy likes to pop up on the scene when you least expect him). Many of our missions were large and complex and there were times we would plan one thing because of something else, because of something else, and because of something else that needed to happen.

Marketplace

In essence, we built a mission like someone would build a house out of sticks, one stick added after another. While building the house, it becomes evident that we needed to start tweaking things and moving things around to support other challenges. Many times, we would have to say, "Stop, let's erase what we have come up with and simplify this mission. What's the goal? What are we trying to accomplish? Let's simplify things and focus on accomplishing that." KISS.

While growing your group, your success will also take the image of having less and less face time with your original members. Let's look at a few things you can control and forget the things you can't control. First, take a deep breath of fresh air. Whether you are the boss or a rising leader, you can influence these things to happen with those you work with.

1. You have the power to elevate morale.

2. People need to contribute. You can inspire them to do so better.

3. Employees should have regular contact with their "boss."

I believe that when people go to work, they simply want to be heard and appreciated. They want to feel valued. In your daily absence, how can you still build trust up and down the ladder?

With or without knowledge, people actually make a purchase from you every day they come in to work. They buy something from you. It's a nonmonetary transfer of funds. They, like me and you, have a deep desire to be happy and content. This need for happiness, or let's call it morale, must be filled in each person.

As their leader, you should use every single interaction to build their trust. As their leader, you should take the opportunity to create procedures and rules that build the trust of your employees. If you're creating silly rules, micromanaging people, or spending your time building a senseless bureaucracy, you'll see that trust dry up.

WHETHER YOU KNOW IT OR NOT, MORALE IS THE INTANGIBLE PRODUCT YOUR EMPLOYEES RECEIVE FROM YOU EACH DAY. Often woven together with trust. What do they purchase it with? Their productivity. Appreciating and leveraging that is an art that once mastered will enhance your leadership during times of growth.

Military Side

The military is a huge bureaucratic engine that depends on policies to keep people productive. There is not always a human leader to depend on to set the tone and atmosphere. So let's take a look at some ways our military has grown a disconnect in the rules they make. Hopefully, you can spot it.

Right now, within the US military, morale and reintegration are two major issues. There is a big push both with legislation and money for our soldiers to be happy and reintegrate back into our normal society after our country has been at war for seventeen years at the writing of this book.

Very smart people have tried to solve the problem of bringing soldiers back from war and releasing them to a successful life in society. Just like our example of building a house of sticks, they have added legislation and budgeted money for the problems, each representing sticks to the house. Reintegration from the military back into the marketplace is difficult because it's reintegrating people from a different culture. Different culture, you ask? Yes, people who serve in the military are absorbed into a military culture. How then is money spent on reintegration supposed to help with that?

How is it that the military is a different culture? One way it is different is the absence of "needed growth." The military also doesn't train leaders how to grow a unit; it expects people to act more as managers instead of capable leaders. If you're given six men to lead, in a year you'll still probably have six men under you. So there is a certain brain atrophy that is formed because growth is not a talked-about objective. In the business world, everything revolves around growth. Growth of your business is what allows bankers to loan you money; it attracts investors. This is a concept unrealized from our reintegrating vets. We think legislation will teach them this detail but it doesn't.

Then there is another factor that widens the gap of keeping reintegrating vets happy. There are leadership skills taught to them that seem good to use, but on the civilian side are time bombs to their success. It's actually a sad thing to me. Military leaders are taught to use fear and anger to get the end result of productivity. IT'S HON-ESTLY THE MOST PERPLEXING THING BECAUSE HERE YOU HAVE ON ONE HAND EVERYONE SCRATCHING THEIR HEADS TRYING TO FIGURE OUT WHY MORALE IS LOW, REINTEGRATION IS DIFFICULT, AND SUICIDE IS ON THE RISE ALL WHILE THEY IMPLEMENT AN ENVI-

RONMENT CONTROLLED BY FEAR. DO YOU SEE THE DISCONNECT? AN INSTITUTION WANTS ONE THING (HIGH MORALE), BUT THEY INVOKE SOMETHING ELSE.

Another legislative disconnect: we tell our warriors to be strong and endure war, yet we expect them to talk about their feelings to counselors at the drop of a hat. It's a bit of an oxymoron.

Enduring war requires you to suck up your feelings and block the horrific. Then carry it with you for your entire life. Yet talking to a counselor or shrink requires you to let it all spill out. That mostly doesn't happen because it goes against what they were trained to do in the first place.

In some situations, when a military member processes out and talks to a shrink, they don't want to talk for a few reasons:

1. The shrink doesn't relate to them. They live the life sitting at a desk. They can't relate to a job that required them to point a gun at someone and pull the trigger.

2. Veterans don't really think a shrink cares. There isn't a "human touch" from counselors. No vet is going to open up about their dark thoughts to them!

3. Veterans believe the shrink is only sitting there listening because they are collecting a government wage paycheck.

If you rationalize it, we expect the impossible of our veterans. We ask them to go to war (a horrible thing to endure) and then we expect them to open up about their feelings (they've been programmed not to) to someone they don't know.

Hopefully, you can see the levels of rules, regulations, and legislation here that don't really address the problems. This leads me back to you. What does your group do to instill a productive atmosphere with or without policy? While you're growing, do you vomit up knee-jerk reactions to solve problems, only to deteriorate trust in the long run? Do people show up for a wage or do they pay for morale with their productivity every day?

Do people trust you?

Biblical Perspective

Sometimes people say that following Jesus isn't cool and it doesn't work for them. I would say that following Jesus is awesome and there is nothing more profitable on the face of this earth than living your life with biblical principles.

Deserving respect, earning trust, building a reputation, being honest and humble at all times—there is no better business plan.

Jesus said it this way, "Seek first the kingdom of heaven and all these things will be added unto you" (Matthew 6:33).

SECULARIZING BIBLICAL PRINCIPLES HAS BEEN DONE SO MANY TIMES, that's because it is the most lucrative way of getting ahead on the face of the planet.

So be careful before you knock it. You might be like me when I found the Lord on the couch of my living room. In the moment that I found God I looked back over my twenty-two young years and was distraught. I couldn't believe that I had to live all those years in the dark. In a few years, you may look back and say the same as me.

Yet I am biased. No. I'm a realist. Following the Lord will never be a loss.

Activation

Ask three people you don't know at your place of work why they come to work. Those you ask will feel appreciated.

BONUS: CREATE A LEGACY

Duplicate Yourself

A leader's legacy is much less about who or what they lead and more about how they lead. Title and responsibilities do not make a leader, but your natural style can.

Imagine the possibilities of the impact you can make if you strive to be a better leader by understanding the emotional and relational qualities you contribute to the people who work for and with you. And when I talk about legacy, we mean what you leave in your wake each time you exit a room.

Each day poses a new opportunity for you to make a conscious effort to connect who they are, how you lead, and what your legacy is and will be.

This book offers many leadership exercises, feedback, and coaching tools to do just that—and keep doing it. Yet remember that building your leadership legacy is a life's work, implemented daily by more than just leadership tools.

So what will you be remembered for? And how will you begin to create it now?

Military Side

This principle reminds me of a common-sense principle each Team guy takes to heart at one time or the other. Crawl, walk, run is what we train by. Each trainee that shows up to BUD/S is not expected to know anything about anything. They are taught each item from its simplest forms. I still remember the first few classes where they taught us how to run. Now, I thought that was a "given" learned at about four years of age. Yet Navy SEAL instructors taught us about the anatomy of the foot and how to step through each step. It was like this with everything we learned; navigating in the wilderness was no different.

SEALs are trained to navigate in the air, on top, and below the sea and in any kind of terrain on earth. Before we are allowed to use GPSs, we have to learn to use the compass.

Navigation on land is a bit different than under the water. On land it's easy. You check your bearing in three different directions and triangulate your exact position. To get somewhere you simply walk in that direction. It can get a little more complicated when it's dark out, but then you just use your last known position and count your steps and use known land features from the map to keep your bearings.

Underwater navigation is more like counting cards in a casino. Just like you have to remember all the cards in a deck, you need to swim for hours without the ability to triangulate yourself on a map.

You have to memorize the dive before you enter the water. You have three items to constantly check while conducting the dive: direction, depth, and time. If you know the direction you're going and how long you're swimming for, you will know when you have gone one hundred meters based on your tempo (speed). For dive safety, you need to always be aware of your depth. You can also use underwater features like marina walls, docks, or the bottom to check where you are. The key is to constantly check your three items of information during the dive. Time, depth, direction. Check the time, check your depth, check your direction, and then do it again. If you're off even a little bit, you'll be off a lot at the end. Throughout your dive, if you make a mistake in your underwater navigation, it could bring you to the wrong target. The same is true in your professional navigation.

During the dive phase of training in BUD/S, one of the guys caught wind that I didn't like being underwater at night. I passively spoke about being on the bottom of the food chain in the water at night, sharks being at the top.

What does underwater navigation have to do with leadership? Well, just like we had to memorize the different legs of a dive before we entered the water, sometimes you just have to wait and get to a point in your professional growth before you figure out what to do next.

JUST LIKE NAVIGATION, YOU NEED TO BE ABLE TO CHANGE DIRECTION AS A LEADER. You need to be ready for anything this life throws at you. If you do the same job and have the same commute for forty years of your life, that's fine if that's what you want. What happens when you need to make a serious change in direction in life and you're too tied down to make the move?

Marketplace

When I owned my CrossFit gym in Washington state, this exact situation happened. There were a few times that some of my coaches talked about opening a gym near mine. A possible future competitor for the same customers was staring me right in the face. At the time,

I was struggling to grow my business and this kind of thing can create fear in most business owners who don't understand this principle of creating a legacy. It was only upon reflection did this principle sift to the top of my heart and mind.

Have you ever had a situation like this? When someone came and said they were going out to do the same thing you are? It is an opportunity often missed in the midst of emotions. With me, I let them know I would love help in any way. I offered to send them away with a handful of clients and some extra equipment too. Free of charge, interest, or a thank you. I believe that offering those to my coaches didn't embolden them to leave my gym and start one; it did the opposite. It made them feel comfortable to be coaching for me. It made them feel a part of the family, but I was only raising up a successor for one day in the future. Yet I was dead serious. I would have sent them with people and equipment. Why? Because my desire was to see them succeed. That's leadership in a good direction.

"But, Charles, if I invest in someone and give all my secrets of the business away, then someone will take those ideas and open a competitor's shop up across the street from me." Well, that might be so, but if your people admire and respect you as a teacher, they won't. If you have a bunch of time bombs still hanging around, then yes, you should fear that.

If you don't fear, your business will stick together and they will want to grow one business bigger than create another one to limp and struggle along. Think about it. PEOPLE DON'T LEAVE A BUSINESS TO MAKE IT BIG. THEY LEAVE BECAUSE OF A SMALL PIECE OF RESENTMENT OR DISSATISFACTION FROM SOMETHING ALONG THE WAY. That comes back to you to take complete ownership of your actions and treat people right—an avoidable time bomb.

Sometimes people will come to you and ask a similar thing about opening up their own shop. If you see the fire in their eyes and they're serious, you may just want to offer them yours and cash out. If you see the passion in their life for whatever cause your running, it means you have duplicated yourself. That's another reason to raise someone up; it makes the passing of the baton an easier process. Just like you see the geese flying south for the winter, one is in the lead for a while but sometimes he needs to go to the back and rest. So it is with business. Sometimes you need to stop leading and move to a position of mentorship. Raising up a successor allows you to do that.

Just like underwater navigation had variations and multiple legs, so does modern-day business. Part of your career plan should be to raise up those on your team and even those you compete with, believing in integrity and karma that all good things will come back to you.

Biblical Perspective

This chapter was first named "Duplicate Yourself." But that seemed so "short-term" and selfish. So I added to it, 'Create A Legacy' so as to take your mind off of yourself and onto others.

If you now or have ever faced the same situation of hearing someone else taking your secrets and plan to open a business location next to you, you have to ask yourself a question. Do you really trust God?

Bringing up someone underneath of you is great for your base. You've got to know that if that ever happens to you, basically have someone who is ready to come up underneath you. Examples in the Bible are so clear.

Moses brought up Joshua, King David brought up Solomon, Elijah brought up Elisha, Jesus brought up the disciples, and Jesus said, "Even others will come after him and do greater things."

SO DON'T BE AFRAID TO BRING OTHERS UP UNDER YOU; TRUST IN GOD. GROW YOUR LEGACY.

Activation

If, while reading this chapter, you have been visualizing some-one who you think would one day be a good successor, your search is over. If not, start asking loaded questions. It's an overlooked part of running a group of people, but you'll find it to be very rewarding to watch someone excel at what you did too.

ABOUT THE AUTHOR

Charles hasn't always been a leader. Most of his principles are not learned through experience but observation. As a young Navy SEAL, Charles was led by multiple military leaders. As a man of God, Charles reads biblical stories with each new day. But his lessons learned in these three areas have shed the light on these thirty-one principles supported by all three perspectives.

Charles currently lives in the Dallas area with his wife and four children. His passion involves finding business opportunities where he can make an impact on culture in a positive way as well as speaking to groups of people to change the culture of leadership in our world.

Charles relishes the opportunity to come to your group and bring tangible encouragement, focus, and life-changing change of direction, steering away from disaster and toward success.

Whether it's schools, teams, churches, corporations, or personal mentorship, Charles is passionate to help.

Why?

Because he cares.

Stop by and say hi to him at CharlesCrouch.com

CPSIA information can be obtained
at www.ICGtesting.com
Printed in the USA
BVHW081325251022
650240BV00002B/88